HAUNTED RIVER TALES

FIVE –HUNDRED YEARS ON THE

LOCHA-HATCHEE

Patrick S. Mesmer

Cover art by Theodore Morris
www.floridalosttribes.com

FOR INFORMATION CONTACT:
Yesterquest Productions
5663 S.E. Mitzi Ln.
Stuart, Florida 34997
1(772)223-5482
pmesmer@comcast.net

THIS BOOK IS DEDICATED TO MY
WIFE TRICIA, MY FAMILY, AND ALL OF
THE FRIENDS AND ACQUAINTANCES
WHO HAVE ENCOURAGED ME IN THIS
PROJECT, AS WELL AS THE NATIVE
AND AFRICAN AMERICANS, UNITED
STATES SOLDIERS, VOLUNTEERS, AND
PIONEERS WHO GAVE SO MUCH.

ACKNOWLEDGMENTS

Steve Carr: Thank you for your tireless support and encouragement, as well as your creativity in developing the characters in this book, and your vast knowledge of anything historic and passion for fun.

Glenn Bakels: Your devotion to the Battlefield is inspiring, and your knowledge shows your passion for history.

Richard Procyk: You're tenacity and no-nonsense approach to history is, in my opinion, the main reason we have this park today. You will be remembered here for generations to come.

Palm Beach County: The Park staff's help and cooperation in this work is greatly appreciated.

Michelle Moore: Your assistance in this project was invaluable.

Patricia Mesmer: My inspiration

Edited by Steve Carr and Michelle Moore

Epilogue by Steve Carr

CONTENTS

Patrick S. Mesmer

CHAPTER 1

CASITOA

Ceremonial Secrets - Theodore Morris

Night Ceremony- Ho-Bay

The year 1513

The warm ocean breeze carried the scent of salt and sea through the gently swaying palm trees. The bright fire illuminated the area in an orange light that highlighted the painted faces gathered around it. The voices sang in unison; haunting chants thousands of years old. All of the men of the village had formed a circle around the fire, with the women and young girls forming a larger circle around the outside. All of their eyes were fixed on a lone figure in the center. Several of the men were beating drums of pulled and dried alligator skin in a slow cadence with the chant, while others shook rattles made of turtle shells in a more syncopated rhythm. The tall shaman stood, his arms raised above his head holding a large, circular object above his head. On his face he wore a frightening mask made from the wood of a cypress tree, the face dyed a stark flat white. The eyes were wide and glaring with red stripes running both horizontally and diagonally out from them. The nose was elongated and oversized, the mouth painted in a small oval. The shaman's hair was long and flowing with osprey feathers fixed to the top of the head at different angles. The object he

3

held over his head was a death mask made from grass and mud pottery clay, its front surface decorated into the likeness of a pig-like creature with the same stark white face; its eyes painted slits, its mouth a round, tight "o" as if it were trying to emit a terrible sound. Two ears stuck up on each side of the face. He danced with slow, deliberate movements in time with the rhythm of the drums while jerking the strange effigy backward and forward over his head. As he danced he moved around the space, alternately thrusting the object toward the onlookers.

The shaman raised his hand and the drumming abruptly ceased. He looked around at the onlookers menacingly and began to speak in a low, growling voice.

"The voices from the trees call to me. They are the messages from the elders. They tell me that the time has come to join the Gods in the stars. They tell me that we need to hold council with them this very night."

The soft sea breeze stirred his long jet black hair as he spoke, and the fire blazed and crackled as a log shifted in the flames.

"We will ensure that we have much sustenance and power over our enemies. We will feed upon their bodies to consume their power!"

Everyone in the crowd was visibly stimulated by this sudden outburst. They jostled and spoke to each other in agreement.

The shaman looked around above the heads of the crowd as if searching for someone.

"Oh great bird spirit! Bring the drink!" he shouted.

Casitoa slowly made her way to the open area of the circle. The smooth curves of her body and the swell of her chest under the loose shift made it clear to everyone that this masked figure was female. The wooden mask she wore had been carved into the shape of a bird-like creature. The face of it was dyed the same stark white as the shaman's and had a large protuberance emerging from its center that was bright yellow, representing a beak. The eyes were large and accented with opposing black lines, giving the mask a startling expression of anger. The feathers of an osprey stuck up from her hair in a half circle around the edge of it.

Around her neck were three sacred necklaces made of dyed clay beads, pierced arc shells, and sharks teeth.

In her hands she carried a small clay bowl containing a thick black fluid that had been prepared earlier by the sages of the village. The drink was made from a mixture of the dried and crushed leaves of the cassina plant and several other ingredients that only the holy men knew about.

Casitoa somberly walked into the center of the circle, pausing when she approached the masked figure. She raised her head and looked into the tall, menacing face, being careful not to look directly into its eyes. She knew that the eyes were one of the three main souls, and she did not want this forbidding holy man to steal hers. She slowly lifted the bowl in a gesture of offering. The shaman stared at her a moment, then bent down and set the grotesquely painted death mask at his feet. With one hand, he raised the mask that he wore to expose the lower half of his face. He took the bowl from her hands, raised it to his lips, and drank. After a few moments, he pulled his mouth away from it.

"Aaaiieeee!" he shrieked, and shook his head back and forth violently.

He put the bowl back to his lips and began to drink more of the liquid. As he did this, the crowd resumed their methodical chant. First the young men in the circle sang one section of the ancient song, and then the women at the rear answered with the next. They had all sung this one many times before, and knew the sequences and variations by heart. The holy man walked to Casitoa and handed her the still quarter full bowl. She took it from his hands and began to back slowly and deliberately toward the breach in the circle.

As the people sang, the holy man hopped in a jerking dance around the circle. His long, shiny black hair bounced in the air behind the terrible mask. The licking tendrils of the fire grew brighter as the wind seemed to pick up slightly. Casitoa, still clutching the bowl of the remaining black drink to her bosom, made her way to the back of the crowd. All attention was on the holy man now as his body and mind began to react to the hallucinogenic effects of the black drink. He shrieked and howled, running from one edge of the circle to the other, frequently losing his balance and nearly stumbling in the sand. The night had seemed to grow darker, and the temperature had dropped a few degrees. The wind had definitely picked up, and the clicking sound of the shell weights on drying fish nets could be heard during the periodic pauses of the song. Casitoa looked up at the night sky and frowned beneath her osprey mask. She sensed that something in the night air had changed, and she felt a sinister fear creep into her mind.

She looked back toward the edge of the palm trees in the distance, and was startled to see a white figure standing by the sea grapes. It stood out starkly against the blue of the sea and the darkness of the night. It was very still and its skin, or some sort of clothing that it wore, flapped gently in the sea breeze. After the initial shock of the sight, she realized that it was a spirit. Fear and dread crept into her soul at the sight of it. She had seen them a few times before. This lonely figure was one of the entities that her grandfather had warned that she would periodically encounter during her life. It was strange to see one now, though, during this ceremony with all of these people about. She then remembered that she alone could see the spirit; others could not. It seemed to be watching the ceremony with melancholy passiveness.

She turned her attention back to the people and saw that the ring of onlookers around the fire had parted, leaving another wide gap in the line. Two stout warriors were escorting a huge man in, pushing him along roughly. There was something familiar about him, but she couldn't see his face clearly in the firelight. His hands were tied tightly behind his back, and he nearly stumbled as one of the guards pushed

him roughly toward the center of the circle. He was much
taller than any other man in the tribe and seemed to tower
above his captors. His dress consisted of only a single animal
skin breach cloth over his private areas. His hair was tied to
his head in a tight bundle, and his entire body was covered
with tattoos of animals and symbols that she did not
recognize. On his face were more intricate displays that
curled around his mouth and up around his eyes giving him
the look of some sort of devil. His tightly muscled body
glistened with perspiration, and he seemed to exude an air of
arrogant defiance, even in his present dire situation, and
glared insolently at anyone who dared meet his eyes. Casitoa
felt a stab of recognition, and terror came back to her as she
stared at the strange, haughty expression on his face and
remembered their first encounter.

He was a member of a rival tribe from the north who
had been taken prisoner after a skirmish a few days earlier.
She had seen him restrained in a small house at the far end
of the village. The strange man had sat for days with his head
hung low, not making eye contact or speaking a word. She
had come to the house out of curiosity to see how different
this unusual man was from her own people. As she
nervously approached the doorway to peer in, she

accidentally stepped on a twig and snapped it. His head had jerked up at the sound suddenly, his face meeting hers. This so startled her that she nearly fell backwards. His eyes were liquid black, and held a look of pure malevolence and hatred. His mouth was twisted in a contemptuous sneer, and he spoke in a low tone.

"Your medicine man will offer me to your Gods, but I will have the last word. My Gods will punish your people for eternity. I say this as a curse on you and all those like you!"

She had turned and run away from the strange, hateful man. She could hear his mocking laughter as she ran.

She had traveled to the winter hunting ground that very night and asked her grandfather's spirit about him, but the old one could offer only scant advice and a sad shake of his head.

"My child," the spirit of the old man had told her, "he is from a people who believe that their own destiny is the only way. This is the nature of all man, and it will be his and our undoing."

The two warriors forced the huge man to his knees in the sand and backed away. The holy man approached and began to dance around the prisoner in a threatening manner. He moved very close and then backed off, waving his hands around the man's bound body. The chanting grew louder and the wind started to blow harder still. The holy man suddenly threw his hands into the air, sending the signal for the two warriors to take hold of the prisoner's arms. The strange man struggled against them even as they dragged him across the sand to a large rectangular stone that rested on the eastern edge of the circle. The prisoner cried out in unrecognizable words of angry defiance as he was again pushed to his knees and his face forced down onto the surface of the stone. The holy man danced with glee as he surveyed his prize on the altar and raised his face to the sky. He screamed with joy to his gods for this moment.

He reached down behind the altar and gripped something. Casitoa knew well what it was before she saw it. It was a war hammer made from a heavy chunk of cochina and tied to a thick cypress wood handle with a leather thong. The holy man stood back and brandished the weapon to the crowd. The chanting had transformed into wild cheers and screams. He very deliberately and ceremoniously raised the

11

weapon over his head. The prisoner shrieked with rage from the altar below him. Suddenly the entire landscape was illuminated by a huge arcing lightning strike and a crash of thunder. The crowd was abruptly silenced by this and stared at the holy man in dumbfounded wonder. He paused momentarily, as if in shock, but soon regained his composure. He raised his arms and glared defiantly back at the crowd.

"Never have the sky elders given us a stronger sign!" he howled.

Casitoa closed her eyes.

The holy man took aim and, with all of his strength, brought the war hammer down onto his sacrifices head with a crunching thud.

Casitoa looked back toward the trees where the ghostly figure had been. It was gone.

Backwoods Hammock- _Jackie Brice_

Jeaga Winter Hunting Grounds

The old man stared at her. She noticed the wrinkles of skin around his eyes as he seemed to squint. She gazed back at him, struggling to maintain eye contact. His mouth seemed to be chiseled into a permanent scowl.

"Grandfather, please tell me what you saw in the water."

13

He said nothing at first. The old man was fairly withered and bent with age. He leaned on a cane fashioned from a smooth branch of cypress wood about three feet in length. He was dressed in a dazzling white deerskin robe, and his whole body seemed to shimmer with a bright light. She noticed that his once black hair was now streaked with the grayness of age. It was tied in a bundle at the top of his head, wrapped around a conch shell, as was the custom of the men of their tribe. He broke his gaze and lowered his head, as if considering her question. After a moment he lifted his eyes back to meet hers. She felt an overwhelming sense of peace and love wash over her. As he spoke the corners of his mouth turned upward in a rare smile.

"Casitoa, you are my favorite child. Your mind is constantly searching for answers. You need to be patient with me. I can see into your soul and I know that you are restless and yearning for answers."

His image momentarily appeared to waver, as if bending slightly, then immediately straightened out again.

She blinked her eyes and felt her temper rising.

"You are teasing me, grandfather. Tell me," she said.

"Casitoa, you have always been impatient," he said. "Even when you were a child I knew that you had your ancestor's stubbornness. Today I looked into my second soul in the water and had a vision that both pleased and disturbed me. I saw many years of prosperity for our people in this place. Our river will provide for us as will the big water to the east. The elders of the earth will see that we will be the keepers of this place for many generations to come."

Casitoa smiled at these words. "This is very good news, grandfather."

"That is not all I saw, young one. In my vision I witnessed the coming of a tribe of strangers to our home. It is my belief that they will come from the big water toward the east. Beware these intruders, young one. They will bring nothing but pain to our people."

"Grandfather, the spirits that I see in the forest, are these the strangers you speak of?"

He smiled at this.

"No, my child, those are the spirits of the lost and wandering. You can see them because I can, and you are my blood and the closest to me. They will always come to you for some sort of warning, usually when you least expect it. You must never try to speak to them, for they cannot hear you. Theirs is a journey that only they can take. You can only see them."

"But they seem so lost, grandfather. It makes me sad to see them."

"No, my young one, do not look at them with pity. This is a great gift that you have been given. They will find their way eventually."

"Why is it a gift? It seems more like a curse, grandfather."

"When you see a spirit, Casitoa, you must be wary because a warning has been given to you from the other world. Something bad may to happen to the people around you when you see it."

Casitoa changed the subject.

"These strangers you speak of; when will they come?"

"You have seen them already, my child."

She bowed her head at these words and recalled a memory of pale, dead eyes.

"No one can dominate our people, grandfather. We are too strong to be defeated by any tribe."

"Casitoa, my young princess, you must learn that, throughout the history of the world, one people cannot rule forever. These intruders are different than any of the others. There is always a stronger tribe that eventually dominates the weaker ones. Today is our day; but that will change. We will anger our gods and pay the price of not being cautious or heedful of our ancestor's advice."

"Grandfather, you know that I need your advice every day. Please do not talk like this."

"Goodbye young one. I must go to join the animals in the forest. Do with my words what you will."

Casitoa reached out toward the old man as his image started to fade.

"Grandfather, wait!"

Her eyes fluttered open. As she regained her awareness she realized that she had been dreaming. Her grandfather was indeed gone. She now remembered that the old man's tired, physical being had gone to join the earth elders many seasons of the moon ago.

She raised herself up on her elbows and looked around. She was in the forest near the place where he and her other ancestors were buried. She had come there from the village near the big water early that morning to consult with them. After spreading out her thatched mat next to the sacred mound, she had fallen asleep. She now got to her feet and looked around, admiring the cypress and oak trees that grew up from the wetness of the swamp. She took in the beauty of the moss that hung down from the branches of the trees and swayed with each gentle breeze, and the large, ornate air plants that nestled in their limbs.

She ran a short distance to the edge of the river and peered into it at her soul reflection in the water. She had bronze, very clear skin with dark, almost black hair, and there were two white stripes painted under her eyes as was customary for a young woman of importance. A single turkey feather hung from her hair. Around her neck were two necklaces; one strung with pearls from the big water, and one that bore three medallions made of silver. The latter was salvaged from the strange wrecked vessel that she had found two years earlier. Its hold had contained a large amount of the shiny material, and her people had considered it a sacred gift from the gods.

Her body was well shaped and strong and her face had very attractive features, with high cheekbones and a small nose. All of this made her very much admired by the men of the tribe. She wore a shift that had been woven from the moss that hung from the oak trees near the main village. Noticing that it was not clean, she brushed some leaf fragments from it with her hand. Casitoa was well aware of her status in the tribe and always wanted to look her best, so she was very conscious of her appearance and tried to maintain it at all times.

She looked up at a great cypress tree on the other side of the river, and her eyes found a large cluster of twigs, grass, and mud that had been built high in the tree's branches. She saw movement in the top part of it and spotted a form that she recognized. It was her favorite bird; an osprey. The creature seemed to gaze directly at her as it let loose with its high pitched cry. Casitoa waved at it as she would a close friend.

"I am not here to hurt you! I love you very much!" she called out to it.

It then dove out of the tree into the air and swooped down at the water, its talons snatching a small mullet from the water with graceful efficiency. Casitoa watched in fascination as it carried its catch back to the nest to feed the hungry young ones. She believed that her grandfather often took the form of an osprey to better watch over her.

She knew that she was going to face disapproval from her mother, who had warned her many times not to venture into the winter hunting grounds. There were many dangers there and Casitoa knew it. The hunting grounds were an important source of food for the people in her village, as well as a welcome and comfortable place to stay during the season of the cold winds. There were many wild animals here including bear, panther, snakes and alligators. These threats to her safety only made her love it even more. She believed that many of her ancestors were animal spirits.

She soon made her way down the worn path that led back to the village. She ran like the wind, for she had always been strong and fleet. During her adolescence she had regularly beaten several of the boys of the village in daily footraces. When the boys realized that it was not wise to be outdone by a girl in front of the village elders, she had not been asked to join the races again.

She ran as fast as she could, her spirit soaring with exhilaration and excitement at the sacredness and beauty of the forest. She felt the joy of being alive as she never had before. She had seen her grandfather in a vision as clear as the day, and she could not wait to tell her mother. She ran until she turned onto the path that led directly to the village. She smelled the salty, humid air and heard the constant roar of the big water in the distance. She could feel the warm sun on her skin.

She thought of her grandfather often throughout the day. She smiled to herself as she remembered the days when he was among the living. She had been a young girl and had been the old man's absolute favorite. He was a very powerful holy man in the tribe and had the respect and fear of everyone in the village due to his age and wisdom. He was an imposing man well over six feet tall with a powerful physique for his age. When young, he had been a deadly and savage warrior and had taken many enemy lives in battle. Most of the villagers would not even cross his path out of fear and respect.

However, when his little Casitoa was around, he was a different person. His entire demeanor changed. He smiled and laughed and bounced her on his knee. He hugged her tightly and whispered his love to her every day that they were together. This was the same man who would slaughter men in battle with a methodical viciousness and not think twice about it later. When the years caught up to him he had become a shaman and stayed in the village most of the time. This enabled the young Casitoa to spend many hours with him during the day.

He taught her things that he knew, including remedies for different ailments comprising of plants and herbs from the forest and surrounding swamps. He showed her how to converse with animals, how to speak to different gods, and the most important lesson, how to communicate with long dead ancestors and loved ones out at the hunting ground by the River of Turtles. He had taken her up the long trail to this place and showed his methods of appeasing the dead ones so that they would open their hearts to her and share their wisdom. They had spent many happy hours there, laughing and talking, swimming in the river, and chasing the turkeys. Those were the best times of her young life.

By the time Casitoa was in her mid-teen years, her grandfather had begun to show signs of his advanced age. He had grown steadily weaker and had become frail. The other holy men of the village had gone into the forest to find the missing spirit that had left his body and made him so sick. He became so infirm that he could not leave his house. Casitoa watched all of this happen. She was at an impressionable and sensitive age, and to watch his eyes grow dull and his memory fail was painful to her. She was there the morning in the Season of the Black Birds when he had taken her hand and gripped it tightly, his old eyes staring into hers. He pulled her down and whispered into her ear in a weak voice.

"When I am gone, come to visit me at the winter hunting grounds. I am going to join the wise ones. Always remember that you are special. Practice all of the lessons I have taught you, and you will become very important to our people. You are my favorite, Casitoa. My love for you knows no bounds, little one."

With these words, he gripped her hand tightly with one last squeeze and slipped away.

The next day she had watched the medicine men lay his body out on the ceremonial mound at the winter grounds. She had seen them place his most treasured belongings around him, and she had personally placed the sacred necklace around his neck. She had watched them carry the white sand collected from the River of the Turtle and cover him. She had cried and mourned his loss for days and had wandered the forest around the outskirts of the village for days searching for a sign of one of his spirits. She knew that sometimes the soul of a loved one slipped into the form of an animal, so she kept her sharp eyes out for any signs from the creatures of the wild. She walked the beach for hours, the salty warm wind blowing through her hair and the sand squeezing through the spaces between her toes. She would never forget him and all that they had shared and the lessons he had taught her.

That was three full years ago. She had missed him every day since. Comachica, her best friend and lover, had been there for her and had filled most of the emptiness in her heart, but there was still the ache of remembrance in her soul that could never be filled. She had learned to cherish the hours she had spent by his graveside when he actually visited her in her dreams.

She smiled as she thought of Comachica. She would find him when she got back to the village.

Morning on Juno Beach- Jackie Brice

Jeaga Shell Mound Village

When Casitoa approached the entrance of the village, the first thing she could see was the very top of the domed roof of the ceremonial house. It was located on top of the huge mound and was constructed of long bent poles and thatched palmetto leaves. Easily the largest structure in the village, it housed the most important men of the tribe. It was where all of the important decisions of daily life were made. The mound itself was comprised of oyster and clam shells that her people had discarded there for more years than anyone knew, even the shamans, and was so massive that a

25

strong warrior standing on one end of it could not reach its
farthest point with a well placed arrow.

There were numerous smaller dwellings built in neat
rows along the river and around the mound. Most of the
inhabitants were currently in the water gathering shellfish or
working at any assortment of tasks by their homes. Casitoa
made her way down the village's main path and smiled at the
children of various ages that were noisily playing together. A
few small dogs barked and chased them around as they
laughed, shouted, and ran in between the small houses. A
group of about six men were on the beach playing a game
with long sticks and a ball made of wound palmetto fiber.
Down by the water she saw three more men who were busily
fashioning a canoe from the trunk of a sizeable cypress tree.
They were smoothing out the sides of it with sharp tools
made of bone, and had lit a fire in the center of it to burn
away the inside.

She approached a group of women at work under a large
palm frond canopy on the eastern side of the mound near
the beach. Her eyes found an older woman with a regal
manner, Zaritaa, seated on a mat weaving some fabric. She
was currently engaged in light conversation with the other
women, and smiled as she spoke. Her elevated status in the
tribe did not require her to labor like this, but she chose to

put her talents to work to help out and occupy her free hours. She was currently in the process of intricately winding some sabal palm root fiber through a back-strap loom. Zaritaa was extremely adept at this method of weaving rough cloth, and she made the finest in the village. Her fish nets were a highly sought after item due to their durability and effectiveness.

"Oh mother, the things I've seen today!" Casitoa said brightly. "The place where the old ones lie is so beautiful!"

Zaritaa stopped her work and turned her full attention to her daughter.

"Why were you there, young one?" she said sharply, an expression of worry and anger on her darkly tanned face, "I have warned you about traveling to that place by the river. There is much danger there."

"Oh mother. You know how much I love it there. I talk to grandfather."

"Casitoa, you must stop this unwise quest for things sacred. You know that you should leave these matters to the men and the elders."

27

She looked back at her mother, the old anger rising.

"You know that father is not the only one in this family who has power," she said a little more sharply than she had intended, "I feel it inside of me."

"You foolish girl!" Zaritaa said dismissively.

"Your father is the Cacique of our tribe! You should try harder to realize your position and help me to gather offerings for his feast instead of running through the forest like a rabbit. Your father would die if you were to be eaten by some wild creature of the forest out there."

"Father does not even know I am alive!" Casitoa retorted.

Some of Casitoa's observations of her father's behavior and attitude toward his only daughter were accurate. As the leader of the tribe, Pijigini was constantly occupied with its day-to-day workings. Casitoa barely knew him, and he did not truly know her. When she was born, her mother had been assigned the work of raising her, but the added responsibility of being Pijigini's wife kept Zaritaa nearly as busy as her husband. This left her aging father to help out with the child's upbringing. Over the years the little princess had grown much closer to him than she had ever been with either of her parents.

"Your father has many important things to consider every day," Zaritaa said. "He has decisions to make that affect all of us. You must not upset him!"

"He is not the only one who has visions, mother. I share his gifts," Casitoa said smugly.

"Your gifts do not matter as much, young one," Zaritaa said with a frown. "You are a woman, and your place is here with me and the others."

"I will not spend my day gathering food and weaving baskets until my back is bent. I have a different calling. I know this because grandfather told me so."

Casitoa abruptly turned and marched away. Her mother watched her leave, shaking her head with frustration as she returned to her work.

She walked toward a group of several men by the river in the process of cleaning and organizing their fishing nets. She spied Comachica among them and immediately averted her eyes, pretending that she had not seen him. The young warrior noticed her and smiled as she approached.

"My princess!" he said with a bright smile. "How are you this beautiful day? Did you come to see me?"

"No, Comachica, I was just walking by," she said coyly. "How are you?"

She walked to him and sat on a small bed of shells, facing him directly. She had to resist the urge to embrace him because it would have been improper for a public display of affection in front of the other villagers. She had known him her whole life, and was very glad to see him. They had been children playing here on this same ground. At that time, long ago, they had been on equal footing; two children enjoying life's wonders. As they had grown older their roles in tribal society had pulled them apart, but they both remembered the strong bond they had shared when young. Comachica was considered to be a strong warrior and a valuable asset to the tribe. Casitoa admired his physical prowess and secretly hoped that he would prove himself worthy to be a suitor for her hand. She loved him, and he loved her.

"I am well," the young man said. "We are trying to net and spear more fish to make sure that there is enough for the night ceremony. Stay here, I'll be right back."

She watched as he bent and retrieved a spear about four feet long and tipped with a small, sharp arrowhead. The end of it was tied to a twenty foot long, neatly rolled cord made from palmetto fiber. He walked to the edge of the river and began to stare into the water intently. He lifted the spear to a position just above his shoulder and held the rolled cord in his other hand. His eyes scoured its surface for several minutes. Suddenly, he seemed to tense, as his gaze focused on a certain point in the water. He brought the spear back a few inches and, in one motion, hurled it into the water. Its path was so straight and unswerving that it slipped into the water with hardly any sound or ripple of the water's surface. The line immediately went taught and began to jerk violently. Comachica pulled on it with his powerful arms and soon had a very large snook on the shore at his feet. The shot with his spear had been true; it had pierced the large gold colored fish through the center of its body. He placed his foot on it and pulled his spear out. He then picked the fish up by slipping his hand through its gill and carried it back to where Casitoa sat watching. She felt her skin tingle slightly as she watched his tightly muscled body work. She loved the way he moved and the way each motion was deliberate and confident. He smiled broadly at her in triumph as he held the large fish aloft. She felt herself blushing under his direct gaze. He dropped the fish on the sand near their feet.

She stood and reached out, gently taking his hand. She pulled him along and together they walked toward the trees.

"I am performing the black drink ritual at the next ceremony," Comachica said with a serious look on his handsome face.

"I already know that! " She said playfully.

They turned down a rough trail marked by a break in the palmetto scrub. The trail wound its way through the growth for about half a mile, and soon they were out of sight of the village. Eventually they came to a small clearing. They turned to each other. Casitoa looked deep into the young man's eyes, and her voice took on a more serious tone.

"I'm greatly honored to do this for you, Comachica. No one deserves this more than you. You have proven yourself many times over through your skill and your hunting prowess."

She paused and her brow furrowed in frustration.

"I sometimes wish that I had been born a man. My father seems to think that I will break like some child's toy if I do anything. You get to have all of the fun."

He laughed, then gazed at her with soft eyes and placed his hand on her cheek. He pulled her body to his and wrapped his strong arms around her.

"Casitoa, you are the princess of the people. You are the most beautiful creature that I have ever seen, and I'm sure that your father feels the same way. He can't show you the affection that he wants to because of his position. I can tell that he loves you more than anything on earth. That I share with him."

The two young lovers gazed into each other's eyes.

"You never need to worry. I will always watch over you," he said.

With that, he bent and kissed his beautiful young princess. The two young people held each other tightly for a long time there among the palmetto and pine scrub.

33

Fakahatchee Moon- Jackie Brice

Change

The night was brightly lit by a beautiful full moon that illuminated the land like it was almost daylight. Casitoa looked up at the millions of bright stars and smiled in amazed wonder. The warm ocean breeze was stiffer than usual and the waves pounded the sand of the beach with methodical regularity. This was a sound that she loved very much. She walked out to the spot where she had spotted the white phantom figure the night before at the ceremony. She searched up and down the mangrove trees by the beach but could find nothing. She walked to the north about two miles, her mind lost in her thoughts, as her eyes searched the landscape. Just as she was going to give up and turn back, she heard a sound just to the northwest. It came from a clump of palm trees swaying in the ocean breeze. It was a soft moaning that was barely audible over the sound of the waves and wind. She walked to the trees and saw the flash of something white and shimmering in the plants behind them. It seemed to be moving away from her, so she followed it into the mangroves. She found herself on a rough trail that wound around the palmetto scrub. Every time she turned a corner she caught a glimpse of white as it disappeared around a corner just ahead of her. She suddenly emerged into a large natural clearing and found what she was looking for.

On the far side of the clearing stood the ghostly white shape that she had caught a glimpse of at the ceremony a few nights earlier. Fear and dread gripped her at the sight of it. She paused for a moment, and then began to walk toward it. As she drew closer she could see that it did not seem to be whole. She felt the panic inside her grow as she took in the appearance of this terrible being. Its features were clear and distinct, but it was much different than any spirit she had ever seen before. It was deathly white in color and seemed to glow with an unnatural light that reflected off everything around it. She was even more shocked to find that she could see through it as if it were made of water! The thing seemed to be floating above the ground. Its clothes hung in ragged tatters from its arms and torso, and the loose ends swayed in the breeze. Around its waist was a broad belt with a large buckle that was made of a shiny metal material.

Its face had features that were very strange to her, but somehow familiar. The nose was long and pointed at the end, and its cheekbones were high and narrow. It had hair growing on it underneath the nose and on the chin giving it a terrifying elongated appearance. The hair on its head was thin and long on each side and parted in the middle, and it waved in the breeze.

The feeling of recognition grew, and she began to become sure that she had seen this thing before. There were two black, empty holes where the eyes should have been. These spaces were blurry and undefined, but she knew they were looking at her.

"What do you want here?" she said to it.

The strange entity seemed to shrink back at the sound of her words. It moved very slowly with gradual, flowing movements as if it were made of smoke from a fire. It seemed to contemplate her for a few moments. It then raised its hands slowly in a gesture of confusion, the tattered clothing hanging from its thin, bony arms. She could almost see the hint of a smile on that terrible face.

"I have seen you before," she said softly.

Then the memory came back to her. A few weeks earlier she had been walking on the beach a few miles north of the village after a great storm. She had come upon the ruins of a strange vessel that had wrecked and washed up on the beach. This stranger was one among many of dead, twisted bodies that lay intertwined with the broken sandy wreckage. She had spent a few minutes inspecting this one's face up close. The dead man's skin was very white, like the belly of a rotting fish. Its eyes were open and staring; sand clinging to the eyeballs. They were strange pale, vacant eyes. The most shocking thing about them was the color; blue as the big water. Those eyes were the strangest thing that she had ever seen. This man's soul was as blue as the ocean! What kind of people were these? Most of them had hair that grew on their faces, while some had no hair at all on their heads. She wondered what they were like when they were alive.

"I know you," she said. "You need to leave this place. There is nothing for you here. My people cannot help you. You need to find your own way. Go back wherever you came from."

The thing seemed to take her words in. It said nothing as if it were incapable of speech. It just stared at her longingly as if confused.

"Leave me alone, spirit!" She screamed.

The entity still said nothing. It just looked at her and slowly opened its thin, gray, craggy mouth. From it came a sound that at first made no sense. It started as a lonely wail that rose and fell with the sound of the wind and waves. After a few moments of this it stopped. Its face contorted in what seemed like awful pain, and the corners of its mouth turned slightly upward in an almost mocking smile. It began to make a different sound that sounded like laughter. It was a terrible, grating, hollow sound. Casitoa could see into its gaping mouth, and she saw that its teeth were ugly black stumps. The peals of its shrieking laughter filled the air.

"Stop that, Spirit!" I am not frightened of you. You should not be here. My grandfather told me that you are not a man, but the remnants of one! You are no better than a discarded shell or a husk of corn. You must leave and go to your Gods."

With this, the thing stopped laughing and stared at her. It slowly raised its arm and pointed to the center of the clearing.

"What are you trying to say, spirit?" She demanded.

The specter simply looked at her with its vaguely mocking expression and continued to point.

Casitoa felt her fear turn to anger.

"I told you to go. I am leaving, but if I see you again I will invoke the spirit of my grandfather and he will send you to the underworld."

With that, she turned and walked from the clearing. She felt the hollow, soulless eyes on her back as she left the clearing and began her lonely journey back to the village.

The next day was spent in preparation for the upcoming feast and celebration. She said nothing to her family, or even Comachica, of the awful thing that she had encountered the night before. The village was a bustle of activity as the women worked the shoreline for the mollusks, whelk, and coqina shells that would provide the fine fare at the night's activities. Fishermen pulled in giant eels the length of a man, and the hunters dragged in several alligators from the river upstream. Snook and redfish were hanging out to dry, and there were clay pots of sea grapes, palmetto berries, and muscadine grapes. Dugout canoes filled with young men gathering fish raced around the river.

Casitoa felt apprehensive as she thought of the spirit that she had encountered the night before. Why was it here? What message was it trying to send to her? She never left Comachica's side all day, helping him pull in fish that he had hooked with his nets or his harpoon. Just as the sun was starting to descend, there was a great commotion at the center of the village. She left Comachica by the water and made her way there to see what was happening. There was a group of men gathered around an old fisherman who was babbling excitedly. She saw her father there, so she ducked behind a tree where he couldn't see her.

She peered around the tree and recognized the old fisherman as Cumoga, a man she had encountered many times when she was on her long solitary walks. She knew that he had shown signs of strange behavior in the past. He lived alone on the edge of the village, and often left for days fishing miles up the beach from the main village. The general consensus of the men was that he was old and senile, and had outlived his usefulness in the tribe. He now appeared to be very frightened and flustered. She heard her father speak to the man.

"What did they want, Cumoga? How many were there?"

The fisherman spat out his words too quickly in his shaken state, so Casitoa was only able to make out bits and pieces of his story.

"Up the beach about ten arrow flights distance! There are many of them! They are coming from a strange vessel that is so large that they cannot bring it to shore! They are coming to the beach in smaller canoes. Our Gods must be angry with us! They have sent these strangers to kill us!"

The older men all had skeptical expressions on their faces. Casitoa's father shouted "Silence Cumoga, you old fool! We are too many and too strong. I am not going to send my warriors up the beach based on your words. You have been known to tell great stories in the past. These so called "strangers" will not come near us. If they do, they will feel the wrath of our spears! We will wait to see what they do, or if they even exist."

Casitoa could see that the men were not even going to consider Cumoga's story. A voice somewhere inside told her that his story was not a lie. She had to see for herself, so she slipped away from the group and made her way back to her house. Her mother was not there, so she went to the thatch pad that she slept on and pushed it aside. She picked up a small stone carved knife that she had found out on the winter hunting grounds and slipped into a pocket inside her shift. She then went in search of Comachica. She found him down by the river a short distance from the village and pulled him aside. She was relieved to discover that he had not heard anything about the wild tales of the vessel up the beach.

"I am going out to the hunting grounds. I need some time to think."

He looked down at her, his brow furrowed with worry.

"Casitoa, why do you have to go alone? Why can't I go with you?"

"My ancestors will not speak to me unless I am alone. I will be fine. I will return first thing tomorrow. Please don't worry."

With that she embraced him and gave him a kiss.

"I love you, my princess." He said.

<u>Spaniards</u>

She walked up the beach to the north, her thoughts filled with a deep sense of dread. She thought back to the strange events of the night before and of the warning her grandfather's spirit had given her. Were these the strangers that he had told her about? Were they the same hideous people as the spirit that haunted her on the beach? These thoughts plagued her as she made her way to an area where she knew the old man regularly fished. She had waited until dark so she could explore unobserved by anyone.

As she walked, she looked out on the water and took in the beauty of the night. The moon still held most of its fullness and was brightly shining over the water, its light painting silver ridges on the gentle waves. A short distance ahead she saw three low, hulking shapes crawling slowly up the beach. She recognized these forms as giant sea turtles coming ashore to lay their eggs. She walked to the closest one of them, dropped to her knees beside it, and gently began stroking its shell. This seemed to comfort her and help calm her turbulent thoughts.

"Hello, friend," she whispered, "thank you for being such a friend to me and my people. I love you very much."

She sat there for a long while with the giant creatures and gazed out at the sea and the stars of the night sky. She felt that it was sometimes better to be alone with only her thoughts to keep her company. This solitude seemed to help her put all things into perspective, sort things out, and make clearer decisions.

She watched the behemoths continue their slow, methodical trek up the beach. They left wide trails of disturbed sand as they pushed themselves across the beach with their strong, fin-like arms. She eventually got up and resumed her journey. She tried to be silent as she made her way north, and walked as close as she could to the mangroves at the top of the beach in case she had to quickly conceal herself. She narrowed her eyes and searched the beach ahead for movement. She had been walking for over an hour without finding anything, and was almost ready to give up when she suddenly spotted a light ahead in the distance. Her pulse quickened and her heart began to race. She heard what she thought could have been a human voice in the distance. Had she found them? Looking around, she realized that she was very close to the spot where she had encountered the terrible spirit the night before.

"So this is it!" she whispered out loud, "This is what you were trying to tell me!"

She now felt real fear and became certain that something terrible was going to happen this night. She carefully continued up the beach toward the light. As she grew closer, the sound of voices became more distinct. She could now see the glow of torch lights and could make out shapes moving on the beach ahead. The voices were speaking in a language that she had never heard before and sounded very mysterious to her. They were speaking very loudly, laughing and shouting as they dragged heavy objects up the beach.

As she approached the area where the strangers were, she looked out over the water and discovered what the source of light had been. She was astonished to see a giant ship silhouetted in the moonlight, the largest thing that she had ever seen in her life. She immediately recognized it as what the broken, smashed vessel that she had found on the beach months earlier must have looked like before the storm god unleashed her fury on it. She could only stare in bewilderment at the webs of lines, ropes, and sails that were going in every direction imaginable.

She hung close to the mangroves to avoid detection, but continued to slowly make her way even closer. She still could not see what the invaders looked like. She realized that she was trembling and drenched in sweat, and that the sand flies were feeding on her bare arms and legs. She dared not swat at them for fear of being detected by these strangers. Still, she wanted to get close enough to see them.

She thought to herself, "Oh, grandfather! Please come to me and tell me what to do! I am frightened!"

She heard no reply. For a brief moment she considered running back to the village to warn the others. She then remembered the dreadful apparition that had guided her to this spot and decided against it, fearing that she would be leading her people into something terrible. Making a conscious decision to continue, she turned and made her way through the vegetation inland between the mangroves and palmetto trees. She travelled a short distance and then turned north, carefully making her way through the low scrub until she felt she was behind the invader's position. She could tell where she was by listening to the voices of the men speaking to each other in their odd language.

She carefully moved closer, peering through the sea grape branches. The voices were very close now. She pulled a branch aside, and in front of her was one of the strangest sights she had ever seen. It was a view of a large clearing lit by a fire burning in a rough pit in the center of it. She recognized this place as the same clearing that she had visited the spirit in the very night before. She realized then that the spirit had indeed brought her here for some reason.

There were six of them at various positions around the fire. She saw that they had the same faces as the dead sailors around the broken ship. They all had hair growing from under their noses and on their chins. They were short men, much shorter than the warriors of her village, and their skin was very pale in contrast to the dark blackness of their hair. They seemed to Casitoa to be dirty and unkempt. Their clothes were even stranger. A few of them wore oddly colored shirts that looked much too big, and a few of them had large black shiny belts around their waists. Some of them wore sandals that exposed their feet, while others wore foot coverings that looked to her like the skin of an animal. On their heads some wore shiny objects that made them look like turtles. A few of the men wore vests made of the same shiny material. They either sat or stood around the fire on palmetto logs that they had dragged out of the trees. Two of the men had no shirts on. They were very hairy with pale skin. These men were slapping themselves on their bare skin because the sand flies were biting them. They were cursing oaths that she did not understand. They were the most peculiar men Casitoa had ever seen. She gazed at them in dumbfounded fascination.

Suddenly someone grabbed her from behind. A moment of horrified panic shot through her. Strong arms clamped around her and dragged her backwards into the brush. She instinctively fought against her attacker and nearly broke free.

"Whoa!" the man howled and laughed as she kicked his leg with the back of her foot. She was then pulled out into the clearing.

The man who held her laughed loudly and gloated in his strange tongue.

There was an uncomfortable silence as the reality of the situation kicked in. The men stared at her, and began to smile. Their eyes roamed up and down her body. They spoke to each other in low voices as they moved slowly toward her. She still had not seen the face of the man who held her, but she could feel his hot stinking breath on her neck. Two of them moved close, so she let out her best loud animal scream and bucked hard against the man holding her. She was in a rage now. She fought as hard as she could, but this only seemed to amuse these hard men. The other men rose from where they were seated and began to close in on her. Their faces were flushed with bad intent and leering smiles.

All of a sudden there was the loud bark of another man's voice. He walked into the circle. He was taller than the others and much older. The hair on his face was gray, his dress was more ornate than the others, and his tunic was made from the same shiny material that she had seen the other men wearing. He shouted something and the men backed away from her. The strong man that held her straightened up and loosened his grip on her a little. The older man looked her up and down and frowned with thought as he stroked the hair on his chin. He looked as if he didn't quite know what to make of this new prisoner. He questioned the man holding her for a long time. Finally, he issued one last order, turned, and walked out of the clearing.

On his departure the men commenced to grumbling to each other unhappily. The one holding her arms grabbed a hand torch from its place by the fire and dragged her through an opening in the mangroves to another smaller clearing. She was surprised to see that they were not alone.

The torchlight revealed the shapes of three other people huddled together underneath a large gumbo limbo tree. As the big man dragged her closer to them, she could see that they were tied and bound together. It was too hard to see who they were in the bouncing torchlight, but she could tell that they were her people. The man pushed his torch into the sand, produced a length of rope from his side, and proceeded to tie her arms behind her back. When he was satisfied that his knot was secure, he let her go and she dropped to her knees in the sand.

She looked up and gazed upon her attacker for the first time and realized how imposing he was. He was very large and had such a terrifying appearance that she nearly let out a small scream. He had a huge mane of long, red hair that hung down past his shoulders like some sort of devil. She avoided looking directly into his eyes lest she lose her soul to him. She saw that he wore the shiny hard material over his skin, and that the front was pulled open revealing a chest that was covered with reddish hair. Her thoughts raced, and she wondered if he was he some sort of animal that would devour her. She saw that he had very pale skin that was covered with tiny reddish brown spots. She felt a small surge of anger and could avoid it no longer; her eyes rose to meet his. Her heart nearly stopped in her chest. They were as blue as the ocean, as blue as the dead man whose spirit she had seen right here in this very spot the night before! He stared down at her, malevolence burning in them. Unable to control her fear any longer, tears sprang from her eyes and ran down her dirty cheeks. She began to scream her loudest wail yet. This angered the big man so much that he brought his huge hand back and, with a great amount of force, slapped her full across the face. She fell backward into the sand and was momentarily stunned by the stinging pain. The sadness and hopelessness of her situation now became clear to her, so she hung her head down to her knees and sobbed in the sand. He muttered something that sounded like disgust and walked out of the clearing.

Casitoa sat there in that same position for what seemed like hours. She was so frightened that she dared not even look up. She shut their strange voices out of her mind and tried to crawl into herself. She had accepted the fact that her death was in front of her. She heard one of the people under the tree next to her speak in a low, raspy whisper.

"Princess Casitoa! Have you come to save us?"

She now recognized this person as Joba, a young fisherman of the tribe.

"Joba! Who is with you?" she said in a hushed whisper.

"It is Papu and Sufa, my younger brother and sister. We were fishing on the beach back toward the village when they took us."

Casitoa put aside her misery and fear and thought clearly for a few moments.

"What do they want to do with us?" she asked.

"I think they mean to take us away. There were others with us. They have already taken them out to the great canoe out in the big water."

A stab of fear shot through her body as she suddenly realized the intentions of these monsters. They were going to be slaves!

"Do not worry. The villagers will come here soon and rescue us," she said in the calmest, most reassuring voice that she could find.

She remembered the "wait and see" attitude of the elders when she left the village.

Hours passed, and she heard no noise except the gentle, persistent roar of the ocean's never-ending song a short distance away. Unable to even consider sleep, she desperately tried to think of any means of escape. She knew that her anger and fear had to be under control, so she tried to quiet her mind. What could she do?

Her spirits lifted when she felt a small weight in her pocket and remembered the small knife that she had taken from her house back at the village.

"Joba!" she whispered, "Reach into my shift and get the blade!"

The boy worked his way over and turned his back toward her. He worked his fingers around the rough handle of the knife and pulled it from its hiding place. He then moved back toward his siblings and positioned himself so that he could slowly cut the cords that bound their hands. After a short time Joba, Papu, and Sufa were free. The two young ones darted away into the darkness. Joba turned to her, and she saw his silhouette in the moonlight heaving with excitement and relief.

"You have saved us, Princess Casitoa! I will cut you free now!"

He scrambled behind her and began to cut through the ropes.

Suddenly, she noticed movement to her right.

"Run Joba! Someone is coming!"

"No! I will not leave you!"

"You must go now!" she whispered in the harshest voice she could gather.

The boy hesitated for a moment, and then disappeared into the dark vegetation.

Her heart leapt with fear as she saw the tall figure of a man walking toward her across the clearing. She was pulled up from the ground roughly by one arm. She felt her hands being untied. The man then shoved her across the clearing, along the edge of the mangroves, and through the small break in the vegetation that marked the short path back to the area near the edge of the fire. The man laughed into her ear softly, and then crudely pushed her with both hands, so that she fell down to the sandy ground on her stomach. She closed her eyes and began to cry with fear and rage as she anticipated what was coming next. He reached down, grabbed her arm, and flipped her around so that she was on her back. She looked up into her attacker's face and saw, with horror, that it was none other than the terrible red haired man! The malicious look in those terrible eyes betrayed the man's intent; he was going to take her by force! Her mind raced, and she looked around madly for any kind of escape.

Without warning, the red man lunged forward and thrust himself on top of her, his full weight crushing her down into the sand. He smelled of filth and sweat, and let out a lustful growl as he ground his pelvis into her. She felt one of his hands grasp her right leg, and the other clamp over her mouth to keep her from screaming.

For one moment she looked up into the great blue expanse of the night sky and saw her friends, the stars. She tried to climb up to join them in her mind, to escape this terrible beast. Her eyes moved down and she found herself looking directly into those dreadful blue eyes. She thought of the dead man on the beach, and the spirit that had showed itself to her. She sealed her eyes shut and tried to find her grandfather's face as the tears rolled down her cheeks.

The red man grinned at her with a malevolent hatred and lust. She felt the terrible probing hand pulling up her shift for access to her womanly parts. She struggled and fought back with all of the strength she could gather.

Suddenly there was another sound. She heard a loud "thwack" and the man on top of her jerked and shuddered as if hit by some sort of spasm. She looked at his face and saw that his expression changed to one of shocked surprise, his mouth wide open with fear and pain. He made a strange gurgling sound. He abruptly pulled away from her and rolled to one side. Still dazed from the assault, she looked up through tear filled eyes and saw another figure standing over her. She felt a rush of joy as she recognized the commanding figure of Comachica. He had come for her!

In one hand he carried a large cypress war hammer with a clubbed head. His body was covered with glistening sweat, and he was breathing very hard. His face was painted with brightly colored stripes of paint that shimmered in the firelight. His searing gaze was fixed on the red man, his face set in a tight grimace of barely contained rage. She turned her head toward the red man and saw that he could not completely roll over because Comachica's war spear was

57

protruding from the middle of his back. A growing pool of blood had formed in the sand under his torso. He looked up at Comachica and his tone changed to that of a whining, frightened child. Comachica stared down at him with cold hatred in his eyes and methodically raised the weapon over his head with both hands. The red man let out a pitiful wail and raised his hands in front of him for protection. Comachica let out a cry of conquest and brought the club down on its target with all of his strength, it's frightening force catching the red man full in the face and splitting his head like a coconut. The terrible red man was no more.

Casitoa looked around and saw that there were others from the village there too. The two men sleeping by the fire would never wake, because the warriors had slit their throats, taken their eyes, and were stripping them of their clothes. Comachica let out another great war cry and held his war hammer high.

There was a deafening explosion from the direction of the ship. This sound was so terrible that the men from the village looked at one another with fearful expressions. They had never heard such a thing and nearly broke with panic. Casitoa wondered if the invaders had somehow captured the thunder. This blast was followed by the screams of the

Spaniards as they attacked from the beach. Comachica looked at the others and shook his head.

"Get ready. The invaders blood will spill this night."

With this he raised his club and let out yet another cry. The other warriors lost their fear and began to shout in unison. Comachica positioned himself at the trail head and waited, his club raised at the ready.

One of the raiders emerged from the entangled mangroves and Comachica caught him fully in the face with the hammer. The man's feet flew from underneath him and he crashed to the ground on his back, his body unmoving. Many others poured into the clearing as the warriors launched themselves into the fight. Men were running everywhere in the darkness as the confusion of battle increased. Smoke billowed through the trees and the screams of men being injured or killed filled the air.

Comachica grabbed Casitoa's hand and pulled her toward the trail to the beach. He led the way through the winding path as they scrambled away from the main body of fighting. They emerged through the palmetto scrub onto the beach and began to run. Casitoa looked back toward the invaders' ship and saw one of them standing upright in the moonlight next to a blazing torch imbedded in the sand. He was pointing something at them. She heard a "swoosh" sound through the air and heard Comachica cry out in pain. He stopped running and reached down to his thigh. A short stubbed arrow projected from it where it had penetrated his leg. Casitoa shrieked and looked back at the Spaniard with the weapon. Seeing that he was aiming it at Comachica again, she screamed in rage at the invader and sprinted toward her wounded lover. She flung her body in front of him just as she again heard the "swoosh" of the weapon's release. She felt the arrow hit her and pass through her body. She felt a great dull pain and heaviness as she hit the sand. She heard Comachica scream with fury and stumble toward her. She opened her eyes and looked back at the Spaniard who had shot her. He was not standing there. He had just been clubbed by a warrior who had come up behind him after the last fateful shot with the crossbow.

Comachica looked down at her, his tears dripping from his cheeks onto her face. She looked up at him and smiled.

"My princess, why did you do this? Why?"

She looked into his eyes, the steady, dull pain of her wound giving way to reluctant acquiescence.

Her voice came out in a hoarse whisper.

"I love you. I will not watch you slaughtered by these men. You must help our people, Comachica. These men are the ones that grandfather warned me about."

He sobbed as he looked down at her, the blood of her mortal wound drenching his bare legs in the sand.

He bent and kissed her as consciousness left her body.

Casitoa felt herself lifting into the air. She felt all of the pain falling away from her body, and the cool night air blowing through her hair. She looked down and could see the beach far below her. She saw Comachica kneeling over someone or something; a large, dark stain forming under it. She felt a sort of detached feeling; not quite sadness, but closer to resigned tranquility. She turned her head and looked off into the distance. The moon was enormous and the night sky was full of millions of stars that burned with a brightness that she had never experienced. It was the most beautiful sight that she had ever seen. She felt the gift of flight come as natural as walking. Her vision had grown so sharp that she could see the smallest movement of the smallest creatures on the ground below. She turned her head to the side and saw the black feathers of her wing. She had taken the form of the creature that she had loved so much in life; an osprey. She turned west and flew toward the hunting grounds to join her grandfather.

CHAPTER 2

<u>ISA</u>

Ambush- Dave Geister

Seminole Village- Locha-Hatchee

January 14th, 1835

Isa leaned on his rifle and watched from the inside of his shelter as the rain pounded down relentlessly. He felt the same apprehensiveness that he had felt all last night. Something was wrong and he knew it. He could feel it. He had always had this power, even as a young man. He looked over at his wife, Sawakee, a few feet away. She looked into his eyes with that calm trust that she had always possessed. Her dark skin accentuated the white clearness of her eyes. She was a Seminole of the Panther Clan, a woman of the tribe. Her lineage was that of Creek descent. She was with child, *his* child, and had made the whole journey through the swamp without complaining at all. He leaned over to her and kissed her.

Sawakee had dutifully followed him all the way from that near disaster at the northern tip of the big lake at *Pay-ho-kee*. His warriors had fought bravely along with Abiaca and all of the others but, in the end, had been forced to flee. They had put up a much stronger defense than had been

65

anticipated and had dealt the soldiers a vicious blow, but Isa knew that they would come again. The soldiers always came again.

Isa was a large man when compared to the others of the tribe. He stood about six foot two inches tall and towered above most of the full- blood Seminole warriors. He was handsome, with rich olive dark skin and large expressive green eyes. He was lean and very strong from a life of survival in the dense Florida wilderness. He always wore the traditional colorful Seminole clothing, consisting of a calico long shirt with long sleeves and a triangular breechcloth with leather leggings. The full dress was a safeguard against the mosquitoes and other insects that inhabited the forests, as well as protection against the brambles, poison oak and ivy that grew everywhere. He wore beaded garters on his lower legs for both decoration and to protect him from snakebites. On his head was a full turban with a large ostrich feather protruding from the back. His jewelry consisted of a beaded bandolier around his shoulders, a large Spanish medallion on a silver chain, four crescent gorgets on another chain, silver wristbands, and silver earrings. On his feet were the same leather swamp moccasins that all of the warriors wore. Altogether, Isa was very intimidating in appearance.

It had been two weeks earlier on Christmas day, the white man's holy day, that they had made their stand at *O-ke-cho-bee* many miles to the northwest. He and many great fighters including Abiaca, Coacoochie, Alligator, and his own leader John Horse had built a strong defense in a high hammock at the edge of the big lake. Isa and his black Seminole brothers had fought bravely and killed many white soldiers that day. His men had prepared themselves well by cutting the five foot saw grass down so they would have a clear line of fire at the advancing troops. Before the battle, Isa had sent a few scouts ahead to lead the women, old ones and children toward the *Locha-Hatchee* to the southeast. He knew the nightmare that would ensue for them if the soldiers gained the upper hand, and he did not want to take any chances.

As the battle began the soldiers had decided to charge in spite of their poor position. This was a decision that they paid dearly for when the entire first attacking wave of soldiers was cut down immediately. The battle had raged on throughout the day until mid-afternoon. Ammunition stocks grew low and they were outnumbered at least two to one, so they had escaped in the canoes that had been prepared earlier. After the battle, Alligator had started a very heated disagreement with the great medicine man, Abiaca, and had called him a coward. As a result of this confrontation the people had split their numbers. Most of the Miccosukee's had headed due south down the east side of the big lake, while Isa, Halleck Hadjo, and Halleck Tustenuggee's Seminoles traveled southeast toward the Atlantic coast. Those had been desperate hours. They knew the trails, but it was very tough going. They eventually caught up with the scouts leading the women and children and had to move as a larger, slower group. They slept very little and kept moving, never making camp for long. Isa knew where the spot was by the *Locha-Hatchee* and led the warriors toward it.

They had arrived at the river in about a week's time and had settled in as best they could. They all had to cross the one half mile wide slough that protected the place to the north and climb up into the hammock. Some of the people were already there and had all joyfully embraced as the families came in one at a time. Isa felt that they were safe for a while because the trees and vegetation formed a thick hammock by the river. This provided the protection and cover that they needed. The women, children, and old ones were exhausted with many of them falling more and more ill each passing day. The rattling coughs of the sick were an ever-present sound in the camp, and there was not much food. The gaunt expressions on the faces of the people were a source of constant worry for Isa and the other leaders. The warriors shared stories of the battle at *O-ke-cho-bee* in northern *Pay-ho-kee*. Their efforts had been rewarded; they had been able to delay the soldiers long enough for the weaker members of the tribe to escape. Any victory, even a small one, over the white soldiers was cause for celebration.

Isa knew that this was an old place because he had come here with his father when he was a boy. The Indian people had lived and hunted here for a very long time. He knew that the mounds to the southeast of the river were burial and had the remains of the old ones inside of them. His people had marked the grave mounds with live oak trees to keep others away and help the spirits with their ascent toward their gods.

It was near one of these mounds that he had first seen the ghost girl.

Isa had been born in the Black Seminole settlement of Pelaklakaha located about six miles from Okihumpkey, the home of the great Chief Micanopy. Micanopy was the nephew of the great Cowkeeper and was the hereditary leader of the Seminoles. The Chief of Pelaklakaha was

69

Abraham, one of the smartest and most influential of the Black Seminole war chiefs. Abraham had been promoted to "Tustenuggee" status as a "Sense Bearer" in the Seminole tribe. Isa had met the man when he was very young, but had not seen him much in person.

Isa's father, Isaiah, was owned by Micanopy, but was also one of his great friends. He and his people were allowed to settle their own town and farm the land on their own, as long as they provided food and much needed manpower for the Seminoles. The war chiefs had noticed Isaiah's great physical strength and prowess and had welcomed him to fight the white soldiers with them. Another advantage to this decision was the fact that Isaiah spoke English, an invaluable skill when dealing with whites from the north. The chiefs were so impressed with him and his abilities that he was allowed to marry Saya, a member of their tribe. Soon after this union, little Isa was born. The Seminole chiefs looked at this young mixed blood boy as an asset possessing the "best qualities of two worlds with the strengths of both." As Isa grew older he learned that the whites did not look at people with mixed blood in the same positive light.

Isa remembered the days as a child at the village. He loved it there. His father made a great home for them. They lived in a fine house that Isaah had built with his own hands, better than most of those owned by the Seminoles. There was so much for a young boy to do, like learning to hunt with his father, fishing, learning to use his hands to build things, and learning to fight. His father had always told him that he must learn how to be a good fighter. When Isa asked why, his father always said the same thing.

"You need to fight to survive, son."

His father had told him many times of his own youthful experiences as a slave on a sprawling tobacco plantation near Augusta, Georgia. There had been a terrible overseer who constantly abused Isaiah and his brother badly. One night, as this overseer slept, Isaiah and his brother crept into his quarters. They surprised him and, in the ensuing scuffle, Isaah's brother killed the man with a machete in a fit of rage. They escaped the plantation together and made their way south toward Spanish Florida. The slave catchers had caught up to them near the Okefenokie swamp in southern Georgia and had killed his brother on a dark, lonely road. Isaiah escaped and made his way south in desperate flight, traveling by night and hiding by day, stealing what food he could from farms along the way. When he entered Spanish Florida he

71

offered himself to the Seminole Chief Micanopy, and the old Chief had accepted him as his own.

Isa had heard this terrible story many times, but his father told it anyway. He said that Isa needed to know.

"You best watch out for them slave catchers, boy. If you ever see them comin' you high tail it out from dere and hide yoself," he said in his strong Gullah accent.

His mother, Saya, was a strong woman. It was said that her mother was a member of the ancient Calusa tribe, and that her father was descended from the Creek Indians of the north. She had been the strongest influence in his young life by showering him with love and never letting him out of her sight.

It was from her that he had first heard the story of the ghost girl of the mounds at *Locha-Hatchee*. Saya had sat by the fire at night, her face transfixed and animated as she told the story of the beautiful Indian princess who had sacrificed herself for her lover.

She looked at young Isa and said, "The princess still wanders those grounds by the river, ever searching for her lover and protecting the graves of her elders. You better watch yourself when you are here at night! She'll come take you away!"

Isa shivered and said in a trembling voice, "Mama, she sounds so sad! Why won't she go away?"

"She can't, Isa. She has to protect those grounds for eternity. That is her curse. She is all white and shimmering, and you can see her when the moon is full!"

"Forever, mama? Like …always?" Isa looked at her with his large, frightened eyes.

She gave a deep throaty laugh and said, "Yes, Isa! Forever."

Riverbend- Jackie Brice

Twenty-Three Years Earlier

Isa and his father had journeyed to the *Locha-Hatchee* just before the first war with the whites to hunt deer and trap raccoons and alligators. There was a village there of about thirty Seminoles and their families, many of them of mixed blood like he and his father. He was about twelve years of age and was just feeling the beginnings of manhood. Isa remembered how beautiful the place looked to him. There were giant cypress and oak trees on the high ground, and the moss hung down from their branches almost to the roots. The surrounding woods were alive with birds and game.

That first evening they had attended a council dance in a clearing by the river and ate a great feast. This celebration had lasted well into the night with much whiskey consumed by the warriors. Little Isa had even drunk some at the request of his father. It did not sit well, and he had vomited on the ground as the braves howled with laughter. He felt very nauseous and slipped away from the group to lie down. He found a spot near a small swell in the ground, curled up into a fetal position, and soon fell asleep.

He woke to an ethereal silence. He could hear nothing but the frogs by the river and a few night birds. He got to his feet and looked up, gazing at the brilliance of the stars splashed across the great expanse of the night sky. He noticed a movement high up in a tall oak tree to his right, and then a flash of white. He stared at it hard and was surprised to see that it was a bird… an osprey. It was staring down at him and not moving. This unnerved him, so he dared not move himself. The creature's eyes seemed to shine. He felt a tight fear in his bowels and decided to speak.

"What do you want, bird?" he shouted.

The osprey seemed to acknowledge this by moving forward on the branch and spreading its great wings. In one motion it leaned forward and seemed to fall from its perch. With a powerful sweep of its wings, the bird's fall became a graceful, broad swoop, and with perfect balance and timing it landed on the ground, hidden from sight behind some short scrub palmettos a short distance away.

Isa saw a white light begin to emanate from the area where the great bird had landed. This light grew more intense, and he saw something move. He then saw what looked like a person standing up behind the palmetto bushes. The eerie, whitish glow seemed to radiate out from its skin, so much so that it seemed to illuminate everything around it. It stood still for a few moments, and then began to gently float toward him with an achingly unhurried slowness. Not a single blade of the palmetto bushes moved or rustled as the figure passed through them as if made of smoke. Isa realized with horror that he could see through it at the bushes behind.

His young mind struggled to make sense of what he was seeing. It was a woman; a girl, he thought.

Or was it?

His hands were shaking and he could not move a muscle. This was greater fear than he had ever known in his young life; even worse than when he had been lost in the woods by himself for two days a few years earlier. Isa could only stare in shocked, terrified amazement as the strange entity noiselessly glided across the swampy floor of the forest toward him. He knew, at that moment, that he was going to die. Just before it seemed that it would overtake him, the apparition stopped. It was directly in front of him.

The girl-spirit regarded him with an almost calm placidness. Her eyes had no visible pupils, but were just black vibrating chasms that, for some reason, seemed to draw him in. He could only hold her terrible gaze for a moment before lowering his eyes in panic. Everything about her was white, but different shades of it, and the lines of her form seemed to quiver and flow gently as if in a breeze. Her shift seemed to be made of rough material, but was white and translucent like her skin. She had feathers in her hair and wore beads around her neck. Her mouth seemed to hold an almost imperceptible smile. She opened it as if to speak, and the sound that came out was the softest whisper that he had ever heard. It was not loud, but seemed to come from the forest all around him.

77

"Isa."

He recognized his name. The sound of it was almost like a breeze.

Isa fell over backwards in confused terror, hitting the ground hard on his back. He raised himself up on his elbows and stared in disbelief at the strange entity.

"Wha wha wha do you want?" he stammered.

The figure said nothing; it just smiled and calmly seemed to watch him.

"Are you a ghost?" he asked in a very small, frightened voice. He felt himself backing up on the ground with his arms and legs in a reverse crawl.

"Yes Isa, if that's what you choose to call me."

There was a long, terrifying silence, and he felt his bladder letting go.

"What do you want from me?" he clucked in a voice that he didn't even recognize as his own.

"I want nothing from you, Isa. I only want you to know that I have you in my heart. I am your friend."

At these words Isa lost his composure. He leapt to his feet and ran from that spot as if he had been burned by a torch. He ran blindly and in a panic. He tripped once, then again, over some cypress knee or broken log. He expected to be split in half by the spirit from behind at any moment. He could feel that terrible stare from those black holes burning through his back as he ran. He half stumbled into his tent and jumped on his sleeping father.

"Isa! What in blazes has gotten into you boy! You actin' like you seen a ghost!"

"I did, father! I did see a ghost! It was a white Indian girl! She talked to me!"

Isa was talking so fast that his words all ran together. His father looked at him with concern for a moment, and then his face broke into a wide smile.

"Did you pee yourself, boy?" He let out a loud guffaw. "I knew I shouldn't have let you drink that whiskey! You seein' things, boy!"

He let out that deep belly laugh that everyone loved to hear, then rolled over and went back to sleep. Isa lay there the rest of the night in his wet breeches, curled up in a ball and shivering, with one eye open staring toward the direction of the mounds.

Lazy River- Marion W. Hylton

Locha-Hatchee

January 14, 1838

Isa, in his shelter with his wife, remembered that night as the rain pounded on the top of the canvas. Even in his adulthood he knew that it had not just been the effects of the whiskey on his young, impressionable mind. He had seen the white woman, the "princess," that his mother had told him about. It was Saya who made him aware, when he was still very young, of his "ability." He knew that the spirits of the dead existed and sometimes roamed the earth. They

81

appeared to him at different times, usually when he least expected it, and only at night. The first had been the "white lady," but there had been many since. The entities that appeared to him could be in the form of a soldier, a lost friend, or even a family member. They always had the same white, gauzy, specter-like appearance. He had grown used to them, in a sense, but they still terrified him every time they showed themselves. Every time he killed a man in battle, he hoped that he wouldn't see him again in the night.

He had seen so much killing and terrible strife in his life that he had grown jaded regarding the subject of death. He often grew defiant and dared the spirits to show themselves to him. He hated the white soldiers so much that he enjoyed watching them suffer and die in the swamps. This war had been a painful chapter in Isa's life. He had watched as the soldiers had relentlessly run his people ragged. The white chiefs had resorted to utter treachery in their frustration by imprisoning warriors under the white flag of truce. They had captured his friend and mentor, Osceola, in this manner. This act had enraged Isa and strengthened his resolve in this fight. Osceola, Wildcat, and John Horse had all been caught by the soldiers and imprisoned together at Fort Marion in St. Augustine. Wildcat and John Horse had escaped by starving themselves and slipping through the bars, but Osceola had been too sick with malaria to attempt it. He was moved to Fort Moultrie in South Carolina and died of the swamp disease after less than three months in captivity.

Isa worried that his people would be driven into the ground. He had long ago vowed to himself that he would not be sent away to some place in the west that he had never heard of. After the bloody conflict at *O-ke-cho-bee*, he had hoped that he could get his people to the coast and attain passage for them to Andros Island in the Bahamas. He had heard of this place from John Horse himself. It was a wild island covered with dense jungle, but it had proven to be a sanctuary for the tough Black Seminoles, many of which had escaped and were living there already. The British had control of this island, but they didn't have the resources to search for the Seminoles and send them back, and probably couldn't find them if they did. This was the reason that Isa and the others had come southeast instead of going straight south with the majority of the Miccosukee warriors. This land was becoming increasingly hostile to his kind, and the thought of a place to go to be free sounded hopeful. If he could just get his people to the coast there may be a chance.

Isa could not understand why the whites would not just leave his people alone when all they wanted was a place to live and raise their families. As these thoughts raced through his mind, he realized that he was starting to get one of the headaches that frequently plagued him. He leaned back and tried to sleep.

He woke with a start. It had stopped raining and was very dark outside, so he got up and walked out into the cool, foggy night. The fires had burned down to red coals and were smoldering away with thin tendrils of smoke rising up into the darkness of the starless sky. Isa looked around at the shabby, makeshift shelters in the small clearing. He could hear the night creatures of the river singing their familiar haunting songs. An owl gave its melancholy taunt, sending shivers up his spine. His people considered owls very sacred, and their presence was not always a good sign. He had a slight feeling of dread as he walked out to the west edge of the camp next to the river. He felt the night breeze pick up slightly, and his keen ears picked up the hint of a sound. It became something he could understand.

"Isa."

It was his name! He felt a chill run up his spine and the sweat that had formed on his back turn ice cold.

"Who's there?" he said sharply.

He heard nothing, and peered out into the darkness. He felt a small twinge of fright; not fear in the natural sense, but something deeper. He heard the crunch of a footstep off to his right about one hundred yards out in the thick overgrowth of the swamp. His hand shot instinctively to his side and quickly withdrew the hunting knife from its leather scabbard. He brandished it in front of himself and stared into the inky darkness.

"Who's there, I say?" he said again.

He saw the light first. It was the same otherworldly white light that he remembered as a child. It reflected off the plants around it as it moved slowly toward him through the vegetation and trees. He heard the light crunching of footsteps.

"Not human," he thought, his keen senses coming to life, "some sort of animal."

The movements were deliberate and almost silent. Then, she came into view. She glided toward him as if floating across the ground. Isa fell backwards to the ground in overwhelmed panic as all of his childhood fears came rushing back all at once. She looked the same, but different to him. The years had added a different perspective; not to the apparition itself, but to his view of it. He now saw something more terrible than before, something ancient and capable of unbelievable depths of sadness that he could not have even begun to comprehend as a young person. He felt his eyes well up with tears at the sight.

She wore the same spare shift, still wore the feathers in her hair, and the same shell necklace. He looked at her feet and saw that they were bare, but it did not matter; they were not touching the ground. Her face bore that same terrible expression of sorrowful regret, and that same stoic smile. Her eyes were the most terrible sight; they were those same indefinable black circles. Everything about her was white and glowing. There was a sound by her side as something approached her in the darkness. Isa looked down and saw the source of the footfalls that he had heard. As it came into the glowing light he could see that it was the largest panther that he had ever seen. Its fur gleamed in the dull light and its green eyes glinted at him. Isa could hear the almost imperceptible, but terrifying low pitched growl emanating from its huge body. It rubbed against the side of the white lady with gentle affection and looked menacingly at him.

"What kind of magic is this?" Isa managed to choke out, "Why have the elders chosen to torment me, spirit?"

The woman- thing just stared back at him for a long moment. He then heard that same whispering sound on the breeze that he had heard earlier. The spirits mouth did not move, but the words came to his ears.

"Isa, I have chosen you because you can see me. You will know me for eternity, my friend," She moved slightly as a breeze blew through the hammock as if she was made of some sort of cloth, "We share many experiences."

There were a few moments of silence as Isa tried to comprehend what was happening to him.

"Am I going crazy?" he asked out loud.

The spirit again began to speak.

"Your Creator made sure that certain creatures of the earth possessed great healing powers. He loved this creature almost as much as he loved you, Isa. He touched the panther with his power long enough so that his great abilities went into it. He told the panther that when the power had been

87

bestowed fully, he wanted him to be the first to walk the earth. Like the panther, Isa, you are beautiful and majestic. You are very special, Isa and that is why I have chosen you."

Isa shifted on the ground and looked from side to side for a means of escape. He dared not move because of the locked gaze of those primal green eyes.

"Tell me, spirit. What does this mean?" he pleaded.

"We are you, Isa," she said in that breathy whisper.

"You make no sense, spirit." He said.

"We are you, Isa," she repeated.

The figure began to float backwards slowly toward the trees, the panther breaking its gaze on Isa and turning toward the trees on the west side of the hammock. He watched them in silent terror, afraid to speak again. He heard the whisper continue as it moved further and further away.

"We are you, Isa."

Isa's eyes flew open. He was on his back in the shelter. He screamed, and Sawakee reached over and held him in her strong arms.

"Isa, what is it?" she said.

He turned and looked at her with wide eyes.

"A dream!" he exclaimed, "It was a dream."

He pushed her away, got up, and bounded out of the tent. It was early daylight and he could smell the fires burning. The women were out gathering what food they could find for the morning meal. Isa ran to the west of the hammock where he had seen the girl. He looked around for any evidence of the encounter. Sawakee came after him, calling out his name. He fell to his knees and searched the ground for footprints where the big cat had been. He felt certain that an animal of that size would definitely leave huge footprints. He looked and looked again, but could find nothing. Sawakee looked at him, concern showing on her face. He got to his feet and walked toward her. His dark face showed frustrated resignation. In a low voice he told her of his vivid dream. She embraced him and they stood there together by the huge live oak tree in the morning dawn.

The fog was thick in the hammock and the surrounding wet land. The people had risen from their slumber and were moving around the encampment tending to their weapons, eating, re-bandaging wounds, talking, washing in the river, smoking, doing whatever they could to maintain a normal existence. Isa was not worried because there were scouts in the trees on all sides of the hammock to prevent any surprises. He had shaken off the effects of the terrible, vivid dream he had experienced and was trying to come up with a solution to his people's dilemma that made sense.

He took his place in a war council meeting that had formed near a large oak tree with three trunks growing out in different directions. This area was higher than the surrounding land because it was a burial mound of the ancient ones who had inhabited this area by the river in a much earlier time.

Isa knew, from stories that his mother had told him, that these people had once been strong and great in number, and were once so fierce that they were feared throughout the entire area. Unfortunately, they were not able to fight the European diseases and slavery that eventually decimated their population. His grandmother, a descendant of the mighty Calusa, had died from an outbreak of smallpox that had ripped through her village about ten years earlier. Once a few of her people got sick, the plague caught hold and spread through the rest like paper burning. Two thirds of them were dead within six months. The old ones did not understand the concept of quarantine, or that a disease could be passed from one person to the next. They thought that they had somehow displeased their Gods. They would gather their families around the afflicted ones and pray, not realizing that they were helping to spread the disease to the ones they cherished the most.

The war council began with a tribute song to them performed by Pictocha, a very old and wise medicine man. The drummers started a sorrowful beat, and the song began. The medicine man told the tale of the ancient people who lived on this sacred ground for many years before any Seminole warrior ever set foot here. They harvested the bounty of the sea and the forest, and buried their dead in the most beautiful places they could find. They believed that the body had three souls; one in the pupil of the eye, one in the shadow that one casted, and one in the water's reflection.

Pictocha then told a story that made Isa flinch. He told the tale of the Princess who had lost her lover to the whites, and how she was still here to protect the resting place of her elders. Isa had to get up and walk away from the council to hide his tears.

Cypress Reflection - Jackie Brice

Skirmish in the Palmettos

There was a commotion from the east side of the
hammock. This was followed by the loud, thundering sound
of musket fire from the trees a few hundred yards to the east.
Three shots in loud succession coming from the north
echoed through the trees. Isa leapt to his feet and ran to his
shelter and his weapons. Men were shouting their war cries
and running toward the trees. After loading his rifle, he made
his way toward the east side of the hammock in a low,

scrambling run. He could only think of one thing; that the soldiers had found their hiding place.

Isa felt the familiar cold sweat forming on his forehead and beneath his shirt. He became aware that the time had come to implement his battle skills. He had taught himself to control the feelings of dread, anger, rage, and fear that, as a younger man, had affected him before a confrontation. He had learned be composed and calculating when the actual fighting began. He became very calm and quieted his mind to form plans and strategies to defeat his enemy. It helped to remember that these were the ones who had everything and always wanted more, and who wanted to enslave him and take his family. These were the men who thought of him and his kind as no more than animals fit to be sold at auction like cattle and horses.

He would not be beaten by them, and he would never surrender. He loved his native brothers and knew that he was one of them. The great medicine man, Abiaca, had personally fostered him to Tustenuggee warrior status. Abiaca, or Sam Jones as the whites called him, had the right attitude when it came to dealing with the whites and their lies. Isa had heard him speak many times on this subject. He remembered the medicine man's words.

"Don't ever deal with them at all. Just fight them with all of your hearts because they can never be trusted. Let the words of the talk enter one ear and pass through the other like the listless winds."

He made his way into the dense foliage and peered between the leaves and branches for a glimpse of the enemy. He heard more shooting and was surprised by how deafening the sound was. As he slowly crawled through the undergrowth he heard the loud, crashing sound of someone running through plants and bushes toward him. He moved to one side just as a warrior carrying a musket nearly ran him over. He recognized him as Mingo, a man much shorter than himself and a full blood. He and Isa had become very good friends in these past few months of hardship and had helped each other many times in battle. Mingo had not even seen Isa in the underbrush.

"Where are you going, brother?" Isa whispered sharply in Hitchiti, the native language.

Mingo stopped and looked at Isa, his face gleaming with sweat and his chest heaving with exertion.

"The soldiers have come from the east. They surprised us, but our scouts fired on them."

Isa said, "We need to hold our ground, brother. We will show them our strength. Remember, this is our place."

The shots continued, so Isa turned from his friend and made his way further through the thicket. He heard Mingo behind him, following closely. The familiar war cry filled the air as the shooting grew more intense. He came to a crest of raised land at the edge of the hammock that gave him a view of what was happening. He saw men running through the woods in a panic. Many of them were dressed in the blue and white shirts of seamen, and they were running the wrong way, toward his warriors.

"I think they are sailors," he said to Mingo, who had cautiously moved up next to him, "these men are not soldiers."

Isa saw his opportunity, so he raised his weapon and pointed it at the running figures. He observed a small group followed by a man who was dressed differently. He wore the blue of an officer, so Isa focused his aim on him. This man was obviously older and having trouble keeping up with the others. Isa waited until he had just the right angle, and aimed slightly ahead of the man to lead his shot. He sucked his breath in and squeezed the trigger. The weapon bucked against his shoulder and he saw the man jerk back with the impact of the ball that had struck him near his heart. He spun around and fell to the ground, clutching his chest.

"You got him!" Mingo exclaimed next to him.

Three of the sailors slowed for a moment to help him. They formed a small group around his crumpled form, huddling around and trying to help. Isa saw the wounded man wave them on as if telling them to save themselves. The men kept looking fearfully back toward the gunfire and reluctantly moved on, leaving the wounded man to his fate.

Isa and Mingo waited a few minutes until most of the heaviest fighting moved on toward the village. They carefully stepped out of their hiding place and walked to the man lying on the ground. Isa saw that the man was still clinging to life, his eyes wide and full of fear and confusion. His hair was gray and his face was wrinkled and ashen. The first thought that entered Isa's mind was that the man was too old to be out here at all. As he contemplated this, the man began to speak.

"I am gravely wounded. Just leave me here to die."

His voice was a rough rasp and the front of his tunic was covered with his blood.

"I mean you no ill will."

Isa said nothing and stared into the dying man's eyes. The man continued to speak.

"I carry no weapons. I am a doctor. I am not here out of any malice toward your people."

"You are a doctor?" Isa asked.

"Yes, a surgeon. I am here only to observe and assist."

Isa immediately thought of the wounded members of his people who had no medical help whatsoever. This man lying here on the ground, if he lived, could possibly help save some of them. He signaled for Mingo to help him, and together bent down and grabbed the man under his shoulders. They dragged him a few feet to a pine tree and leaned him against it. Isa pulled the man's tunic open and inspected his wound. It was bad, but the blood had slowed some.

"Stay here," he said to the doctor. "We will come back for you."

Isa and Mingo left the man there and moved on through the trees. He figured that by the time they returned the wounded doctor would most likely be dead anyway. If he was still alive, Isa would carry him back to the village and he might be able to help with the injured there.

The firing was growing more intense from the direction of the village. More men were running through the trees now and confusion and panic seemed to be everywhere. Isa lowered his head and stealthily crawled forward through the vegetation to gain a better view. Most of the action was off to the north of his position, so he and Mingo continued a flanking maneuver. They stayed just beyond the edge of the fighting so they could observe it and make the best move. They kept their heads down and kept moving. They could hear the balls whizzing through the trees and leaves and the sounds of men screaming with rage and pain. Every so often they would cautiously look through the brush, only to find some man running in the wrong direction, or one who thought that he had not been observed. Isa was surprised at

the ease with which the Seminoles were able to out-
maneuver the inexperienced fighters. They had stumbled
onto this place and were in the process of being annihilated.

The skirmish lasted for most of the afternoon as the
sailors were scattered and pushed back toward the river to
the east. Warriors were whooping, shooting, and running
through the swamp toward the retreating men. The trees
were full of the smoke of gunpowder. The fighting moved
further to the east, so Isa and Mingo found a secure spot to
rest in a small, well concealed oak grove.

Isa carefully raised his head to look above the scrub
pine at some of the aftermath. What he saw both shocked
and surprised him. Through the wafting fog of the battle, he
saw a black man just like himself. His body was slumped in a
crouched position behind a grove of trees. He was dressed in
sailor blue and white, and was still clutching the musket in
his lifeless hands. He seemed to have been killed while
protecting an officer whose body was crumpled by his feet.
The officer had obviously been wounded in the skirmish and
had died during the battle. The bodies of four dead Seminole
braves and a large dog were scattered around the clearing in
front of them.

Isa and Mingo walked to the grove of trees and stepped over some fallen branches to where the sailors lay. He placed his gun barrel at the black man's head and pushed it. The head lolled back, and Isa could see the gray hair that betrayed the man's age. This man was older than he was. He could see the hole where the ball had entered his brain. He looked into the man's face with fascination. It was obvious to anyone how this situation had transpired. This man had single handedly killed four war-hardened braves and their dog while protecting his wounded commander. Isa could feel no pity, but he did feel admiration at this man's toughness and bravery. He said a prayer that the Great Spirit would see that this man's soul found true rest. He and Mingo sang a death song for the four dead warriors and moved on.

Darkness fell and with it the shooting ceased. The braves had chased the sailors and soldiers back to their boats by the river where the latter had been forced to make a hasty, disorganized departure. Isa learned from one of the returning warriors that these men had been saved from complete massacre by the efforts of one brave, obviously battle experienced white man who had rallied them into some semblance of order and organized the retreat. He had done this after most of the officers in charge had been killed or wounded by single-handedly establishing a withdrawing skirmish line. This gave the remaining men time to load the wounded on the boats and get them away. Many warriors told of how they had shot at this man, only to find that he was not injured. Shortly after the last boat left, it had to return because, in their panic to flee, the sailors had accidentally left this fearless white man, who had saved their hair, behind on the shore.

The warriors were returning to the village laughing, the smiles on their faces showing the joy of victory. Isa and Mingo were walking back toward the village when they came upon the place where they had left the wounded doctor. He was not there. They made their way back to the village and the sounds of celebration. The warriors were doing a victory dance around the fire. They held the scalps of several slain sailors above their heads. Mingo happily joined them, but Isa chose not to join in the festivities. He knew, as all of the more experienced warriors did, that this was not a joyful victory. The men that they had fought were not the main body of the white forces, but inexperienced sailors acting as scouts. He knew that it would only be a matter of time before the real army came to them.

He found the doctor on a travois by the far side of the village with two older women attending to him. The man was in very rough shape, but still alive. He was gravely pale and his breath was coming in labored wheezes. Isa looked down at the man and spoke.

"We have many wounded braves here. You will help them and your life will be spared."

The doctor met his gaze and surprised him with a crooked smile.

"I am not going to survive the night, my friend," he turned his head away and coughed loudly. Isa could see a small amount of blood spray from his mouth on the dry grass.

"I'm a dead man here with you anyway."

Isa studied the white man's face for a moment as if assessing his words.

"No, we need a doctor here. Many of our women and children are ill from the constant fighting and running. I promise you that if you help I will see that no harm comes to you."

The doctor looked off into the distance and shook his head slowly, and spoke in a quiet voice.

"I will do what I can for you."

Isa turned and walked away. He noticed that there was a small group of braves that had formed to his right. One of them seemed to be struggling with the other two, so he approached them.

"What is wrong with him?" he inquired.

"Metetakee is in a bad way. His brother was killed by the whites in the fight and he is very angry and sad," one of the men answered.

Metatakee had his head hung down so his face was not visible but his sobbing could be heard.

Isa said, "Brother, we have all had great losses in the fight. We will have our vengeance, but we have to stay right in our heads."

The grieving man answered him in a shaking voice.

"I hate the whites so much that I want to kill them all now. My brother was a gentle soul and they have taken him from me."

As the man spoke, Isa placed his hand on his shoulder in a fatherly gesture. He felt a great sadness for Metetakee as he wept. He had lost many friends and relatives in the fighting, and it was moments like these that the senselessness of it all it all became clear to him. The relentless onslaught of the soldiers had decimated his people's way of life. He felt tears come to his eyes as he shared the loss with this sad man.

Suddenly, and in one swift motion, Metetakee ducked down and broke away from all three of them. He made a dead run for the edge of the hammock where the doctor lie. As he ran, he pulled a long bladed hunting knife from his sash. He shrieked as he raised it over his head.

Isa cried, "No! Don't do it!"

Metetakee roughly pushed one of the women out of his way and fell to his knees by the doctor. He screamed with rage and, with both hands, drove the blade deep into the doctor's chest.

Days later a dense fog had settled in over the village. It had been quiet, but there was an underlying sense of desperation in the village that seemed to be growing every day. Food stores were running low, so the warrior scouts were searching the surrounding woods for anything that would provide sustenance. Isa knew that the soldiers would not let his people rest for long, so he and another warrior, Halleck Hadjo, had posted scouts at the east and west of the village in a continuous vigil. He knew that an attack by the enemy would likely come soon, but he also knew that he could not ask his people to run yet. There were too many sick and old people, as well as mothers with young children, to make the arduous journey south as Abiaca and his warriors had done two weeks earlier. They would have to make a stand against the soldiers in this place.

Night had fallen, and the only sounds to be heard were the endless songs of the nocturnal creatures of the swamp. Isa opened his eyes. He could hear the soft snoring of his wife and saw the gentle rise and fall of her body as she slept. He rubbed his face with his hands and realized that he had to make water, so he emerged from the tent into the foggy night. He walked to the edge of the hammock and headed down a small trail to an open area in the palmetto scrub. As he did his duty, he absent-mindedly gazed into the trees. He heard a haunting, familiar sound, and his body stiffened. It was the lonely call of the owl, a creature that his people held very sacred.

He felt a growing sense of fear and dread, and tried to scan the darkness of the trees. He suddenly had the feeling that he was not alone. He looked deep into the dark hammock again and spotted something that didn't seem quite right. It was at first a flicker, then a steady light that seemed to be moving through the trees. The fear paralyzed him and he was afraid to stir. It was a figure moving along through the forest; not walking, but gliding. He could hear no sound at all as would be expected with someone or something making its way through the woods on a dark night. As it moved closer to him he tried make out its features. He watched as it floated along and soon realized that it was not headed directly at him, but seemed to be wandering aimlessly. Isa did not make a move or a sound and craned his head up to try and see what it was. He almost screamed out in horror when he found out. He had expected to see the spirit woman, but this was not the case.

Isa realized with shocked disbelief that this thing had once been the doctor. This was the same man that he had shot and then tried to save. He had seen this man brutally killed with his own eyes! It was dressed the same as the doctor had been in life, but the whole body, including the clothes, glowed with a terrible ghostly luminescence. Its mouth was partially open in a grimace, giving the horrific face an expression of hopeless sadness, and its eyes were the same black, empty pulsating voids that he had seen on the other spirits. Its chest still had the huge bloodstain across it.

It floated several inches above the ground and made agonizingly slow, methodical progress across the swampy forest floor. Isa stood in horrified fascination and watched its progress. It soon became apparent to him that this spirit did not seem to know or care if Isa was there or not. He could hear its voice speaking in his head, but it was more of an incoherent mumble. Isa sensed that this spirit appeared to be lost, confused, and hopelessly disoriented in its meaningless quest. It glided right past him in his hiding place by the trees. He waited until the phantom had disappeared completely before emerging into the moonlight.

As Isa walked back to his tent he felt exhausted and slightly nauseous. He bore great sadness and pity for the doctor's spirit in its sorry condition. As he ran the whole scene back through his mind he noticed that his hands were shaking. He had many questions and no one to ask. Why had he been "chosen" by these spirits? Why did he not see "all" of the dead? Why were there only a chosen few of them? Many men had died in the day's fighting. Why had he been shown the sad, wandering spirit of the doctor? What did it all mean? Was he going to die?

Isa made his way back to his tent and crept inside quietly so as not to awaken Sawakee. She was now heavy with child and would need her rest. He lay there the rest of the night staring up at the canvas roof of his tent, unable to sleep.

Anhinga Trail *Jackie Brice*

The Final Stand

January 24th, 1838

The scout came running into the village shouting

urgently. The news was not good. A large contingent of

soldiers was making its way toward their position and was

only a few miles off. The warriors began making their

preparations for the coming battle. The food situation was

very bad and many of the women, the elderly, and the

children were very weak from hunger. As the men got their

weapons ready the women packed up all of the essentials

that they would need for a quick flight from the village. They

had grown much too accustomed to this ritual. Many of the

people barely had enough clothing to cover their bodies and

had to make do with the scraps of cloth that they had left for

protection against the elements. A few children were crying

in the confusion, and their mothers were trying to console

them. They knew that a crying child could betray a person's

hiding place to the soldiers. There was an overall feeling of

fear, apprehension, and weariness. They knew that if they

could not hold the soldiers off that they would be driven out of this place to "who knows where." The escape canoes were made ready on the river.

Isa sat on a palmetto log and cleaned his weapon. Sawakee was hurriedly stuffing their tent canvas and few belongings into a military pack that Isa had taken from a dead soldier at *O-ke-cho-bee* a few weeks earlier. As he gazed at the Spanish small bore, breech loading rifle that he used in battle he felt gratitude that the soldiers, with all of their superior numbers, had inferior weapons when compared to those of the Seminoles. The French and Spanish had been trading weapons to his people for a long time now. The breech loaders were much easier to load, so the warriors could get more shots off in less time than the enemy. The soldiers used muzzle loading rifles that were very inaccurate at long distances. They took so long to re-load that the Seminoles could often overtake them in between shots. The soldiers knew that wet gunpowder was useless in a fight, but many of them were so poorly trained that they didn't even take the necessary precautions to keep theirs dry. Seminoles carried their powder packs in their mouths to keep from losing them or getting them wet. The warriors had developed a tactic in which they went into battle almost naked carrying only their weapons. They did this because they had learned that if they were hit by a musket ball, the fabric of their clothing would create infection.

Isa smiled as he remembered some of the great victories of the past. The soldiers had no idea how to fight here in the swamp. The lines of uniformed men had blundered into their ambushes for years. The great spiritual leader, Abiaca, had called the piles of soldier bodies "blue coat mounds." Another problem for the soldiers was that the majority of them did not do well in the extreme heat and humidity of Florida. Many of them died of "swamp fever," or malaria, general exposure, snake bites, or heat stroke.

If the Seminoles found themselves in trouble in a skirmish they could just melt back into the undergrowth to pre-determined hiding places. They had lived in this harsh environment for years and had the advantage of fighting on familiar ground. They could both attack and retreat quickly and take as long as they needed to re-group. The frustrated white chiefs would coerce one Seminole leader to sign a treaty or an agreement to bring his people in on a set date, only to find out that he only represented a small band and that none of the others would honor the agreement.

Isa knew that the future did not bode well for him and his brother warriors. The soldiers were becoming more and more persistent in their pursuit. They had begun to send in troops from the sea to the east and west. Isa knew that he had nothing at all to lose by fighting with everything he had. If captured, he and his wife and unborn child would either be killed or sent to a plantation in the north as "recovered property" even though they had never been slaves themselves. He would die before surrendering to the whites.

A cry from outside his tent interrupted his thoughts.

"The soldiers are coming!"

Isa leaned over and kissed Sawakee and whispered some instructions into her ear. He helped her up and watched her walk toward the east where the boats were. He had to look away as the reality hit him that he may never see his unborn child alive. He blocked this thought with a curse against his enemy and made his way to the ambush point where the warriors were getting into position. Many of the old ones were wandering around in confusion and there were still children running around the camp. He heard a loud cry from the edge of the hammock. The soldiers had arrived.

Isa heard the "pop- pop" sound of the Spanish breech loaders that signaled the others to prepare for battle. He peered through the thick vegetation of the hammock and saw the skirmish line approaching in the distance. He saw the flag waving and heard the shouts of the soldier's commanders. There was a swampy slew about a quarter mile long that the soldiers had to cross. It was not as wide but very much like the one at *O-ke-cho-bee*. Isa watched as the horse mounted cavalry struggled to get their mounts through the waist deep water. He could see them cursing and pounding their terrified horses to urge them on.

"Fools," he said aloud to no one, "our people chose this place well."

The Seminole sharpshooters fired away, felling several soldiers as they foundered in the chest high water. The horses almost immediately became stuck up to the saddles, so their riders had to abandon them and continue on foot. Isa fired at them from his spot by a grove of pine trees. He heard a sharp cry and looked up to his left just as one of the warriors who had positioned himself high in an ancient cypress tree was hit in the chest with a musket ball. He fell from the tree and landed roughly on some sharp cypress knees at the edge of the river bed. His body lay motionless.

The persistence of the soldiers soon paid off, and they gradually began to gain more ground toward the warrior's line of defense. Isa moved back a short distance to secure a better firing position. He heard a loud, thundering sound from the direction of the attack and immediately realized that the artillery gunners had moved into position at the center of the hammock and were firing a merciless barrage of canister and grape shot directly into the trees from several six- pound howitzers.

Isa looked to his left toward a small open clearing and saw Mingo running toward him from a thicket of trees on the other side. Isa gave him the hand signal to stop and get down, but his friend seemed to be caught in the fear of battle and continued toward him unabated. Isa now urged him on, screaming for him to run faster, but his friend was not swift on his feet. He heard the sound of something ripping through the trees like some sort of huge spinning bullet from hell. Isa was looking directly into Mingo's eyes, as if willing him to move faster, just as it struck his friend in the head, decapitating him instantly. One minute his friend was there, the next his headless, lifeless corpse fell to the ground at his feet. Isa shrieked with rage and shot blindly into the smoke.

At that moment, the thought came to him that today could well be the day that he would walk across the milky way to join his ancestors. He ran back further to the rear, the words of his death song on his lips.

The hammock was now filled with smoke and the deafening sound of gunfire from both sides. Isa and the other warriors hurriedly moved back to a position on the other side of a shallow crossing in the river. As they were changing position they passed the bodies of several dead warriors, so Isa said a silent, brief prayer for each one he saw. They moved to a new location in a nearly impenetrable stand of ancient cypress and swamp maples that provided good cover from which they could fire at the oncoming soldiers. Earlier, they had equipped these trees with gun rests so they could shoot more accurately. As the first soldiers came into view the warriors began shooting.

These were not the bluecoats, but the other whites that were dressed more like hunters and farmers. Isa knew that these men were not part of the main army. They did not fight like the soldiers, nor would they commit themselves like the soldiers did. Isa had seen men like these slaughtered by his warriors in the swamp during the initial attack at *O-ke-*

117

cho-bee. The white soldier chiefs had sent men like this in first to die in the initial attack. He now watched as several of them went down screaming in pain. They were near the far bank of the *Locha-Hatchee* but would not cross because of the withering fire from the Seminole guns. The bluecoat officers were screaming at them to move, but they would not traverse the river. Isa thought that this was probably a smart move on their part. His men would cut them to pieces.

"Better to be cowards," he thought.

With the soldiers advance stalled, the gray-haired chief of the whites soon appeared on a great horse. He dismounted and seemed to plead with the farmer-soldiers to follow him and continue the attack across the river. Their mounted, uniformed leader was a stocky man who seemed hesitant and indecisive about what to do in the face of the heavy fire from the entrenched Seminoles. The gray-haired chief seemed to be so frustrated that he could barely contain himself, and an argument between these two men soon ensued. Incredibly, the chief pulled his side arm and aimed it up at the mounted man's face. After a heated exchange, he ran out into the open area by the bank all by himself, waving his pistol over his head like a crazy man and shouting loudly, trying to urge the frightened men on.

Isa smiled as he watched this brave, insane act. He could see by a glint of reflected sunlight that the old man was wearing spectacles. The idea occurred to him that he would like to see how the foolish man looked without them, so he placed his rifle in the crook of a cypress tree and carefully took aim. He squeezed the trigger and shot. The old man's head jerked violently and his hand shot up to his face. Isa could see that he had not killed the man, but had hit him with a glancing blow to the face. The spectacles flew off into the weeds a few feet away. Incredibly, the man dropped to his knees and fumbled in the grass with his hands to locate them. He picked up the broken frames, and then retreated back out of range of the shooters. Isa thought that this brave, crazy man looked a lot better without his glasses.

The officer's outrageous behavior was apparently the incentive that the soldiers needed to hit the water, and they ran at it with a vengeance. At the same time, a ways to the south, several screaming, saber wielding mounted dragoons had appeared and were fast approaching the warrior's position. Isa knew then that the battle was lost, so he ducked under the cover of some bushes and reloaded his rifle. He scrambled back to the east through the thick, overgrown vegetation, then made his way south around the approaching dragoons.

He was making his way along the river when he heard a familiar noise from a short distance away. It sounded like the loud bawling of an infant! He cautiously stood and peered over the bank. There, on the far side, he saw one of the bluecoat soldiers standing in shallow water next to a young girl holding the crying baby. Isa immediately recognized her as the daughter of one of his warriors. The soldier's right hand was on the girls arm, and the left held his musket. It looked as though he were trying to pull the girl from the water. Isa's mind went red with rage, and an image filled it of his own unborn child in the hands of the whites. He let out a scream of anger and rose up to his full height, pointing his rifle directly at the soldier's head. The soldier turned and looked straight into his eyes.

All time stopped as Isa realized that the soldier was a very young man. He did not see hatred in the boy's eyes, but something else; compassion, fear, and something else; tears. It was too late, though. Isa squeezed the trigger. At the very same time, the young man wildly swung his musket up in his direction. Both weapons roared almost simultaneously. Isa saw the red blot of blood on the boys exposed forehead and the eyes roll up into his head for the last time. At the same time he felt the dull, thudding pain in his chest as the small lead ball entered it. He turned and made a mad run into the brush away from the river. As he ran, he felt the searing pain of his injury start to grow. He looked down and saw that his bare chest was covered in blood, and he could see the wound pumping blood out like a small gusher as he ran. He smiled cynically as it occurred to him that the boy had made a very lucky shot.

He ran until he was far away from the battle. He continued to run until he felt his body weaken. He found himself at the river again and followed it south, his breath becoming much labored, his chest and stomach soaked with blood. He saw Sawakee and his unborn child in front of him, but knew that they were not really there. He tripped on a cypress knee and stumbled headlong into a swampy section of arrow root and mud at the edge of the *Locha-Hatchee*. Rolling over onto his back, he gazed into the sky. The girl spirit was there, smiling at him. She did not look so terrible to him now. She smiled and extended her hand out as the darkness overtook him.

Isa bounded through the forest. He felt wonderful. He was more agile than he had ever been. He felt a great joy at being there; at being alive. He felt different, but not uncomfortable in his new skin. His hearing had become very acute, and he found that he could hear the leaves dropping from the trees and the squirrels foraging in them from a great distance away. He was very hungry. He saw the river that he loved a short distance away, so he walked to its edge and drank from the cool clear water. He raised his head and looked at his reflection. He had transformed into a beautiful, golden panther.

CHAPTER 3

<u>WILLIE</u>

U.S. Soldiers- <u>Dave Geister</u>

"A lengthened trail ye tread, my braves,

and difficult its sign;

Through hummock and through everglade.

By marsh and tangled vine."

Patten

Fort Pierce, 1838

The reflection of the late afternoon sun on the surface of the river cast a wondrous mosaic of tiny brilliant lights against the blue- green of the water. A young blonde-haired man of twenty-one years sat on the sandy beach gazing out at the beautiful view of the Indian River. His soldier-blue trousers were rolled up halfway to his knees and his feet were bare, his toes buried in the cool sand. The January breeze felt good blowing through his hair and around his ears, so he had unfastened the buttons of his tunic to allow it

125

to ventilate his upper body. His handsome face was set in determined concentration as he held a smooth, round glass bottle wrapped with fishing line tightly in his hands. The line led into the water directly in front of him about twenty feet beyond the shore. "I reckon this must be the finest day on God's green earth," he said to the dark haired boy sitting next to him, "I do declare it, Josiah."

Josiah grunted in agreement. He was smaller in stature than Willie at about one hundred-fifty pounds and had a thick shock of black hair that continuously fell into his face whenever he wasn't wearing his leather forage cap. He was a good looking boy, but he had a slightly pinched face with small black, darting eyes that made him appear to be in a constant state of nervousness. He now lay back on the beach with his legs fully outstretched.

Willie's fishing line was taut, but not yet tugging with a prize. He looked around at the other young soldiers who were sitting up and down the beach and smiled. Slowly pulling the bottle back, he teased the bait. Suddenly there was a small jerking tug; then another. The pressure became steady and the line went very tight, dipping down toward the sand of the beach. He let out a "woo hoo!" and jumped to his feet, gripping it tightly. Several of the other young men clapped and shouted words of encouragement. He applied even, steady pressure to the line as not to break it.

"This is a big one!" he cried out.

He moved back, further up the beach, constantly pulling and winding the line around his bottle, trying to gauge the size of the fish that he had not yet seen. He was able to get it in a little closer, so he rolled in more of the slack. Walking closer to the water's edge, he kept up the even pressure. The line tugged and jerked with the tension of the fight. He had caught the interest of every boy on the beach as he pulled in his quarry. He rolled and spun the bottle madly as he tried to make up the slack.

"This is the biggest hog o' the day or my name ain't Willie McCracken of Coker Creek, Tennessee!"

"Pull her in, Willie!" Josiah shouted.

Willie soon won the battle with his reward jumping and slapping on the beach.

"A sweet redfish!" Josiah exclaimed.

"Dinner'll be a durn sight fine tonight, thanks to me!" Willie shouted.

Josiah said, "This place is so fine I believe I could live right here directly. To hell with them Indians!"

They all laughed at this.

Behind them the log picket fence stood as a looming testament to their past few days of hard work. They had been toiling non-stop since they had climbed ashore after their river trip in the large flat bottomed boats from St. Augustine, many miles to the north, a week and a half earlier. The officers had no sooner stepped on the dry sand of the beach when they immediately set to work choosing the best location for a fort. The site that they eventually chose was a high bluff a little ways to the north with a natural fresh water spring running down the south side of it making it an ideal place to build. The soldiers had performed the hard labor of cutting trees and dragging them in from the flat pine prairie forest just to the west. They had then stripped them, cut them to the proper length, and started the construction of the first blockhouse about twenty-five feet from the edge of the bluff. It took many trees to do it, but their little army had plenty of manpower. They soon had a fine fort complete with a two story blockhouse, large parade ground, officers and regular quarters, and a small hospital at the southeast of it. The officers had named the place after their leader; Lt. Benjamin K. Pierce of the 1st. Artillery.

There was a good sized force of Navy men that came down the coast with them in small boats under Lt. Levin Powell. They called themselves the "Waterborne Expeditionary Force." Willie and the soldiers called them "swamp sailors." They were a mixed lot with nearly every other one of them being a Negro. There were several officers and a few civilian professionals traveling with them, but Willie didn't know their names. He and the other soldiers stuck to themselves and looked out for their own, and so did those navy boys. There were about eighty of them in all, and they made camp down the beach to the south of the fort.

Lt. Powell was to use his waterborne force to traverse the interior rivers and streams in search of the Indian camps. Another one of his goals was to try to find a water route to the huge lake named *O-ke-cho-bee* many miles to the west. The army had obtained information that many Indians were hiding out there on its small islands. The Lieutenant liked to travel the river at night because it was cooler, and his men could spot the glow of Indian campfires in the distance. This force had left a few nights ago heading south in their flatboats like a tiny armada.

After a lot of backslapping and congratulations the boys heard the shouting of the Sergeant-at-Arms back inside the fort. Willie picked up his fish and he and the other boys climbed the embankment. As he walked, he looked up and noticed the large mound that was located by the south side of the fort to the southwest of the hospital building. It was about forty feet in diameter and was about thirty feet high and covered with small trees and vegetation. The officers had chosen to build the fort just to the north of the spring that ran alongside it.

"Lord that thing is huge. What manner of injun you reckon put that there?" Willie said out loud.

"I don't know, but I heard tell thay's bones buried in it." Josiah said.

Willie said nothing, but his thoughts were very active. He had seen other mounds like this one in various places along the coast during their march into northern Florida. He wondered about the people who had lived there. The questions were always the same. Who were they? What did they do? How did they survive the sick season here? These questions were always there in his mind, and often helped him occupy the long hours of boredom of army life. Putting these thoughts aside, he followed the other young soldiers past the small hospital building, through the opening in the picket fence, and into the fort parade ground toward the company barracks at the south side of the fort.

Later that night, as they were sitting by the fire after their delicious fish dinner, Willie brought up the subject of the mound again.

"Who do you think the Indians were that built that?" he asked Josiah, keeping his voice down so the others wouldn't hear.

"I don't rightly know, Willie", Josiah answered. "I reckon it was some tribe of headhunters like the ones in Africa that I learn't 'bout in school when I was a welp."

Willie's eyes widened at this.

"Head hunters?" he asked quizzically.

"Y'all don't never know", Josiah said. "Could be they hid some o' them heads right there in that mound."

Willie lay awake in his tent thinking most of the night. He missed his home back in Tennessee. He had a young wife, Susan, who was doing her best managing their small farm in his absence. He had a little boy, Billy, with thick blond hair like his own. He missed them both so much that his heart ached with loneliness. He cursed the day that he had ever joined the army for this miserable war in this miserable land. Why would any man want to conquer this place? Why didn't they just let the Indians have it? This place here by the water was acceptable enough, but for the most part, the place was a swamp. He had never seen more worthless land in his life. He didn't hate the Indians as much as the others; he felt bad for them. He had seen whole families of them starving to death near St. Augustine. Yes, the Seminole warriors had attacked white farms in Georgia, but they had been provoked, in his opinion. He actually admired them for their toughness and their uncanny ability to survive in this godforsaken swampy wasteland. He thought of them raising their families here in this tough place. This was their place. They were raising their children and burying their dead here. He thought of the mound off to the south of the fort. Were there really bodies buried in it? If so, were they Seminoles? He didn't think so. The mound was way too old for that. He could not get it out of his mind. He had to inspect it closer.

The next morning he was awakened by the bugle at dawn. He and Josiah went through the usual series of morning drills with the other soldiers, and then ate a breakfast of huge oysters from the river. Later, in the barracks, he bent and picked up his pack, pulled it over his shoulders and walked outside. Later, when there were a few minutes of idle time, he and Josiah slipped away and walked down past the many tents of the soldiers. They nonchalantly made their way along the picket fence rails across the parade grounds to the gate, which was open during the day. They walked out of the fort and across the ground to the south. Jumping across the spring creek, they approached the north side of the mound. They looked around behind to make sure no one had noticed them, and hurried around to the back side of it. It was heavily overgrown with weeds and small trees and bushes.

"Now we'll see just what's buried in this here hill. Follow me," Willie said.

"We cain't be too long here, Willie. The Sergeant'll be lookin for us to work on something afor long," his friend said, looking back toward the fort.

"Ah, hush up. We got at least an hour and a half."

They climbed about halfway up the mound where Willie saw a spot of sandy earth that was free of large bushes. Willie turned to Josiah and smiled as he pulled the small folding shovel out of his pack. He dropped to his knees and started to dig in the sugar sand, and soon had a hole about a foot down and roughly a foot wide. In the bottom of it he saw a harder, rough surface. He pushed the sand away with his hand. It was a hard packed layer of shells mixed with sand. Josiah looked on from his standing position behind him.

"Whheeeuh! That ain't gonna be easy to bust through!" Josiah said, laughing.

"Ahh, this ain't nothing," Willie said as he raised the blade of his shovel and stabbed it into the shells. It slid in about halfway, and he scooped it up and dumped its contents to the right of the hole. He dug down through the hard surface about another foot, the sweat showing through the shirt on his back. Josiah fell to his knees and started to dig himself. Soon they had a larger hole that was about two and a half feet deep.

Willie suddenly raised his hand. "Wait!" he said in a sharp whisper.

He had seen something that did not seem right. He reached into the hole and pulled gently up on the object. It moved, and then something next to it moved. It was a shell, but it was tied to other shells with some sort of string or cord.

"A necklace!" Willie exclaimed. "It's wrapped around something."

He reached into the hole with his bare hands and began brushing sand away. His fingers moved over an object that was very uneven in texture. He had found something else.

"I'll be damned, Josiah. Its bones! Real bones! There's somebody buried here; a body!"

Josiah immediately recoiled in horror.

"What in hell are you doing, Willie? We need to leave that alone!"

"What's the matter, Josiah? This is what we came to find."

"Maybe you. Not me, I'll warrant. This is grave robbin'. I ain't no sinner."

Willie felt his anger growing.

"Ah, hell, Josiah. Why don't you just go back over to the fort where it's safe, then."

"Well, maybe I will then. You're gonna burn for this, Willie."

With that, Josiah turned and walked down the slope of the mound and back toward the fort.

"Say hello to the other women, and let 'em know yer souls in good standin!" Willie shouted angrily.

He snorted in disdain and turned his attention back toward his find, his curiosity getting the best of him. He could definitely see the shape of what looked to him like a ribcage. He used his fingers to dig out more sand and shells from around it, and he soon unearthed what appeared to be a jawbone. He carefully dug further up and around the object and after several minutes had the entire skull exposed. He rested his weight back on his legs and sat up. Willie looked down at what he had found and shook his head in amazement. He couldn't believe that he had actually found a body. An idea occurred to him then. He gazed at his find in the hole for a few moments, and then reached down with both hands into it. He placed a hand on each side of the skull and, clutching it tightly, wriggled it back and forth until it came loose in his hands. He raised it up and gazed into the vacant eye sockets, a foolish grin on his face.

"You're coming with me, Charley."

With that, he turned and grabbed the cloth sack that he had brought with him and gently placed the skull inside of it. Turning away from the hole, he started to get up. He paused, as if in afterthought, and turned back toward his find.

"Almost forgot," he said to himself, "something for the missus."

He reached back into the hole, clutched the shell necklace, and stuffed it into his bag. He backed away from the hole and got to his feet.

Suddenly, there was a series of high shrill cries from the trees behind him on the other side of the swale behind the mound. Whirling his head around and up toward the trees, his eyes met the late morning sun, temporarily blinding him.

There was a great, mad, black whirl of commotion directly over his head that seemed to come from out of nowhere. He felt something smack into his head, and then felt the pain of something digging into the skin of his scalp. He panicked and immediately raised his hands in fear, and began beating at the thing with his fists. Whatever it was shrieked madly and dug deeper into his scalp, and he felt the sting of blood seep into his right eye. He made contact with the thing with one of his wild swings and felt it break free of its grip on his head. In the confusion, he tripped on a clump of grass. He felt himself losing his balance, and he started to fall. He tumbled hard to the ground and then rolled to the bottom of the mound, head over heels.

Willie lay there dazed and completely terrified for a moment, sprawled out on the ground, not quite comprehending what had just happened to him. It occurred to him that he had just been attacked by some sort of wild animal. He got up to a kneeling position and looked wildly around for a sign of his attacker. He felt his head with shaking hands. He found two gouges in his scalp under his hair about five inches apart. They were cuts, but they were not too deep. He had blood running down from his face and around his ears. His mind began to clear and he considered the situation.

"Some sort of damn crazy bird." he said aloud.

He heard the cry again and quickly dove to the ground in panic. He peered up toward where he thought the sound had originated from. He saw it then. From its perch about thirty feet high in a pine tree there was a large bird; an osprey. It had black, cold eyes and seemed to be glaring directly at him. Willie looked back at it, an unnatural chill forming on the skin of his back. It was staring at him! The bird lifted itself from the branch and took flight. Willie took two steps back in fear. Why was this happening? What had he done to anger this creature? Was he near a nest or something? The osprey flew in looping circles in the sky about two or three hundred yards up directly above the mound area.

Willie's fear now began to be replaced by anger. He felt rage at the audacity of this animal. He looked around the ground and found a good sized rock. He picked it up and, with all of his might, threw it at the creature. It didn't even come close to its mark and just bounced off a branch. The bird continued flying in its pattern and shrieking.

"Damn you bird!" he cried, shaking his fist in the air. "I'll kill you! I'll eat your damn babies if'n I find 'em!"

With that he climbed the hill and retrieved his bag. He strode back down the side of the mound and turned toward the fort. He stopped at the stream and, kneeling at the water's edge, cleaned the blood from his head. He would be too embarrassed to tell Josiah what had happened, so he pulled his soft leather forage cap from his sack and pulled it over his head to cover his wounds.

It was then that he heard the horses coming. Looking up, he saw a few mounted soldiers emerging from the Indian road on the west side of the fort. They were dusty from the dry trail and they appeared to have come a long way. As he watched, many more filed in, two or three at a time. Soon there were what seemed to be hundreds of horse-mounted soldiers pouring in. They spread out in the clearing south of the fort as they came in. There were so many that they stretched out a considerable distance southward. Many of them rode down toward the water and immediately dismounted, walking down the beach and stretching their tired muscles. Willie nodded greetings as the tired riders rode past him. A few officers gathered together at the south side of the fence and rode into the parade ground together. Next, the infantry men started to march in from the west along with several horse-drawn Dearborn wagons.

Willie knew that this was Hernandez's mounted dragoons and infantry force. He and the others had heard that these men were soon to arrive, so the activity was not a major surprise. The men were laughing and cajoling each other, obviously glad to be here in this place rather than out on the rough terrain of the Florida plain. They were so hungry that they devoured the fish that were caught as fast as they could be brought in.

The next few days were a bustle of activity around Fort Pierce. Colonel Pierce himself and a small force of men went north in boats to the "haul-over", an area to the north by Fort Anne where the boats had to be physically dragged over land to the Mosquito Lagoon because there was no direct inlet to the ocean, to procure provisions from St. Augustine.

The very next day another large force of soldiers and mounted dragoons came in from Fort Lloyd to the west. These were General Jesup's men, accompanied by the 2nd mounted Dragoons and close to six hundred civilian volunteers from Missouri and Tennessee. Jesup was the commander of all of the military forces in Florida. He was an older, humorless man who seemed to always look annoyed. Willie supposed that the man had a stressful job and was

under a lot of pressure to get the Seminoles to agree to leave
Florida and go west to the Oklahoma territory. All of the
previous commanders had failed to have much impact on
the battle hardened Seminole warriors up to this point in the
conflict. Jesup's reputation had taken a hit when the
northern newspapers had reported the news that he had
captured the great leader Osceola under the pretense of a
white flag of truce. Willie imagined that the man wanted this
war to be over; the sooner the better. There were now over a
thousand men at Fort Pierce. Willie knew that something big
was going to happen very soon.

He was down by the water with his bottle fishing rig
when he was approached by one of the soldiers from Lt.
Jesup's command.

"Howdy. Name's Private Wayne Henderson of
Moorehead, Kentucky. How's the fishin?" the soldier asked
in a friendly voice.

"Not so good, this mornin'," Willie answered, "Not sure
what the problem is."

Wayne looked at him. "What in God's name happened
to your head?"

Willy answered, not looking at him. "Durn crazy bird attacked me. I think I was too close to the nest or somethin'."

Wayne laughed a little at this. "Damn, boy! She took a chunk out of you!"

He looked out at the water and sighed. "I wish I was back home. I love to fish. I got a big lake right near my farm."

Willie smiled at this. "I wish I could go with you. I loved fishin' back home." They both looked out at the river and said nothing for a few moments.

"Wayne, have you heard anything about when we're movin' out of here?" Willie asked.

The soldier looked straight at him and said, "I know that things are getting' hot. We just heard about Colonel Zachary Taylor's troops out at *O-ke-cho-bee*. They had a huge fight with them savages on Christmas Day."

Willie stared intently as the young soldier gave his account of what had happened.

"Seems that a good number of men met their maker that day. Ole "rough-and-ready" sent them Missouri volunteers in first right into direct fire. They said ole Sam Jones was there, and Wildcat, Alligator, John Horse, and all the toughest ones they had. Taylor eventually won the day, but not without takin' some heavy losses. I sure am glad I wasn't there. After the fightin' was done the Indians ran for the canoes and high tailed it out of there."

"How many men were killed, Wayne?"

"Twenty-eight dead in the swamp," Wayne said matter-of-factly, as if he were recounting a hunting trip, "and over a hundred wounded."

This information sent a chill up Willie's spine. He shared the same fear that all of the other young men felt; the prospect of dying here in the swamp at the hands of bloodthirsty savages.

That night Willie and Josiah were bedded down in their tent in the parade ground down near the entrance of the fort. They talked for a while, keeping their voices low.

Josiah said, "Do you think we'll be movin' out soon?" He paused for a moment, looking off at nothing. "Seems to me like these Generals are gittin awful antsy for a fight."

Willie looked over at him pointedly. "I don't know. I just want to get movin' and get this sorry job done so's I can git back to my boy before he's all growed up."

Willie did not tell his friend about his conversation with Private Henderson on the beach earlier. He knew that Josiah had not seen much actual fighting and was very nervous about the prospect of actually fighting Indians.

"Willy, can I ask you somethin'?"

"Yeah, I reckon."

"Did you find anything in that mound yesterday when that bird attacked your head?"

Willie was feeling rather embarrassed about the whole mound adventure. His head wounds hurt and his muscles ached from the fall he had taken. Both he and Josiah were wearing their forage caps strapped around their chins. They slept with them on to keep the centipedes and caterpillars, not to mention those huge cockroaches, out of their ears as they slept.

"Nope, Josiah. I thought I found somethin', but it was just an old animal carcass." he rolled over on his side. "Go to sleep, Josiah."

Glades Moon- Jackie Brice

The Dream

His eyes opened and saw the roof of his canvas tent. It seemed strangely quiet. There was a sound off in the distance that he could not recognize. Was it some kind of bird? It was like a singing wail. He sat up and looked outside of the tent through the opening. He heard Josiah's even breathing as he slept. Making his way out of the tent, he breathed in the cool, damp night air. He was amazed at how quiet it was. There were a thousand men here and he couldn't hear a

sound. He looked up and sucked his breath in at the sight.
The stars were brilliantly lit and larger than he had ever seen
them. He noticed that his head did not hurt now. His hand
instinctively reached up to feel his wound, but he was
surprised to find that it was not there! For some reason he
did not think this queer. There was something very different
about this night. He looked down toward the river and could
see everything. He could see the bright full moon reflecting
off the water and the palm trees swaying gently in the breeze.
He felt very strange and lightheaded. He walked through the
parade ground and out through the gate of the picket fence,
then made his way between the many white tents that were
set up all along the riverfront. He walked slowly and
deliberately, enjoying the feel of the cool breeze off the water
blowing through his hair. He walked far down the beach
beyond any of the soldiers or the horses and eventually
found himself in what looked like an abandoned Indian
settlement. He remembered the place because he had seen it
earlier that week on a previous hike. It looked very different
at night. The scattered poles left over from the Indian homes
jutted out of the ground and took on a whole new looming
appearance in the stark moonlight.

He felt fear slowly building inside of him. Something
was not right. There was a sound from the east, so he turned

and looked. At first, he couldn't comprehend what it was he was seeing. There was a light moving toward him from across the water. As it glided closer to him Willie saw that it had the yellow amber radiance of a lantern and was chillingly beautiful against the dark blueness of the night sky. It was as if it were from some other world that Willie had never seen or even comprehended. It's terrible beauty mesmerized him, and he could not move; he could only stare at it as it approached, his stunned terror growing.

It appeared to be a woman!

No, a girl! What was it?

Her entire figure seemed to smolder with that amber glow, and the loose shift that she wore wafted lightly in the breeze. Willie now tried to scream with all the force that he could muster, but his throat was silent. He seemed paralyzed as a new level of sickening fear overtook him. The ghost girl was getting closer, but her legs were not moving, and Willie realized with horror that she was gliding across the top of the water. Her head was slightly cocked to one side, and her arms were open as if welcoming him. There was no movement of the water's surface beneath her.

149

He could see that she looked Indian, but like no Indian he had ever seen before. She was tall and the dress that she wore seemed to be made of a very rough material. She was very well formed, but not entirely…..human. Her face was the most terrible thing he had ever seen. It had the features of a beautiful young woman, but with two large black empty holes where her eyes were supposed to be. Her mouth opened and closed slowly and Willie could see that the inside was as black as a pit. He felt a pang of terror as he saw a large spider with long angled legs emerge from it and swiftly crawl across her starkly pale face. It climbed over her shoulder and disappeared around her back. He heard a sound that sounded like laughter all around him, but not from the figure itself.

"Willie."

It was his name. Something or someone was calling his name. It sounded like it was part of wind, like it came from the very earth itself.

"Wha wha what?" Willie stammered out loud.

He heard it again.

"Willie."

He found his voice all of a sudden. "What do you want?" he said in a voice that came out quieter than what he had intended, like a squeak.

He felt like he was under some kind of spell. He was more terrified than he had ever been in his entire life, but he could not move at all.

"You are not a bad man, Willie." the barely audible voice said.

He could not reply. He began to turn away to run, but suddenly felt like he was up to his neck in water. He was moving so slow!

"Why did you take them, Willie?"

He heard it, then; a question. Or did he? Was this demon spirit from the water asking him a question?

"Why did I take it?" He mimicked the question as if searching for confirmation that he had actually heard it.

"You know, Willie."

All at once it came to him. It was the skull and necklace from the mound. This spirit had come to punish him for stealing it. He felt warm tears spring from his eyes and run down his cheeks.

"I'm sorry! I didn't know!" he blurted out toward the desolate wraith now standing no more than twenty feet in front of him.

The spirit's mouth took on the form of a smile. The great black eye holes seemed to pulsate with fluid definition.

"Willie, you are me. It is too late. You have already angered him."

Willie felt like the last bit of sanity was starting to leave him. He was crying like a baby now and shaking with fear.

"I'll put them back!" he screamed, "I didn't mean no harm!"

The figure was starting to turn away. Willie felt panic setting in.

"Wait! I'll put them back tonight!"

He heard a sound coming from the mangroves on the west side of the beach, and noticed that one section of them was moving. He saw that same awful amber luminosity that had surrounded the ghost girl glowing above and through them. Something was coming for him. He turned and began to run, but his movements were, for some insane reason, agonizingly slow and arduous, as if he were completely submerged in water. Slowly, agonizingly, he tried to force his movements as fast as he could, but was only able to generate a labored struggle. A scream filled his lungs, but nothing came out, and his eyes frantically searched the beach to the north in front of him for a glimpse of someone coming to help him. He strained to put one foot in front of the other and felt as though he was running into the wind of a hurricane.

He heard heavy footsteps running in the sand behind him. Whatever unearthly beast was behind him quickly closed the gap between them, and then let out a loud, almost human, scream of rage. Willie knew, at that moment, that he was going to die. He thought of his wife and son, and that he would never see them again. Directly behind him, he heard a great grunt of exertion, and something hit his back with extreme force. He then felt the most excruciating pain that he had ever experienced. He looked down at his abdomen just as the stone point of a huge spear penetrated it, jutting out in front of him in a burst of torn skin, blood and gristle. He tried let out the pained roar of a wounded animal, but again, no sound came from his mouth. He felt the awkward weight of the spear throw him off balance, and he began to fall to the sand.

His eyes snapped open as he was jolted out of his heavy sleep by a loud explosion. His entire body was drenched in sweat. He sat bolt upright and realized that he was still screaming. Josiah was staring at him from his bedroll with wild eyed confusion.

"What in hell's got into you, Willie?

Willie could only stare at his friend, a shocked look on his pale face.

"You been moanin' for almost an hour now. I thought you was sick or somethin'!" Josiah said.

"It must have been a nightmare!" Willie said out loud.

"You don't say! I thought you was dyin' over there, Willie!"

"Oh Josiah, I am so damn happy to see you."

Josiah just stared at him, a skeptical look on his face.

"Now you're really scarin' me."

Willie looked out of the open flap of the tent. He could see that it was still dark outside, but there was light emanating from many fires. He heard the voices of many men singing and nattering in boisterous conversation.

"What in hell is goin' on out there, Josiah?

"Aah, it's some of those durn Alabama and Tennessee volunteers. They dun got into the whiskey and a few of 'em are all liquored up and shootin' their guns in the middle of the night. There'll be hell to pay in the morning with the officers."

Willie flopped down on his back and closed his eyes. He soon fell into a deep sleep and dreamed no more that night.

Sun through the Pines- Jackie Brice

Swamp Sailor's Misfortune

He awoke the next morning to the sounds of men shouting. Josiah's neatly folded bedroll and pack lay in the space where his friend had slept. Outside, there were soldiers walking and running everywhere, and the fort seemed to be a bustle of activity. He sat up, undid the chin strap of his cap and removed it from his head, and temporarily enjoyed the slight cool breeze that blew over his sweaty scalp. He knew that he had slept too late, but he reclined again and stared at the tiny holes in the canvas roof of his tent. The memories of the night before came flooding back to him all at once.

He had never had a dream that had seemed so real. He had never experienced anything like that in his twenty-one years. He was sure that he had actually been killed by some great demon spirit out there on that lonely stretch of beach. He turned his head and looked at his cloth bag. He contemplated its contents and wondered about the possible connection between them and that terrible dream. Was he going crazy? He reached over and picked it up, hefting its contents with one hand. Just as he was about to open it and look inside, Josiah poked his head in the opening of the tent, startling him so much that he dropped the bag.

"You'd best get your durn self out here before you get kicked!" Josiah hissed loudly. "The officers are all fired up this mornin'. Lt. Powell's sailors got back last night, and they are in a bad, bad way!"

"What do you mean, Josiah? What happened?"

"Just git out here! I'm serious!"

Willie leapt to action and scrambled around the tent, getting his things together. He had no time to worry about the bag that contained the skull and necklace; he needed to get himself out and in line. He emerged from the tent and stood fully upright in the morning sun. It was a beautiful January morning and the fresh breezes from the river blew through the palmetto trees by the beach causing their long fronds to sway gently to and fro. Willy looked out at the river and, shaking the off the gloomy memory of the night before, realized that this was probably the best weather that he'd ever experienced.

It didn't seem fair to him that this swampy, desolate landscape could be blessed with such a desirable climate this time of year. He knew that the summers were definitely not nearly as hospitable. The army did not fight in Florida during the "sickly season" months. The risk was too high of the soldiers contracting maladies ranging from malaria to general heat exhaustion. Also, the mosquitoes were so thick that they could suffocate a man.

He straightened his tall forage cap, patted his faded blue uniform and straightened the white cross shoulder belts that supported his cartridge box. He checked his scabbard and gun sling as he walked down toward the river. He had never seen so many men in one area before. There were fellow soldiers, volunteers dressed in civilian clothes, Indian scouts, officers dressed in every manner of uniform, sailors in pea coats, and many others. He hurriedly blended in with a group of regulars as they made their way through the gates of the picket fence and down to the river where a large number of small boats were landed.

The riverfront was a mass of confusion as many men crowded the shoreline. Many of Lt. Powell's sailors, both white and black, were laid out on the sand and appeared to be badly wounded and bleeding. Many of them were groaning and writhing in pain from their injuries. The soldiers and volunteers were in the process of carrying the most severely damaged men up to the fort. Willie counted close to twenty men lying on the beach. He approached a soldier who was tending to an officer who had been shot in the shoulder. He gazed down at the suffering man and immediately discerned that he did not look good. The officer was ghostly pale due to loss of blood. His eyes had dark circles under them from the pain and exhaustion of his injury and the many desperate hours spent on a flat boat. His head was lolling back and forth and he was moaning something unintelligible. Willie looked up and saw a man he knew only as Sergeant Moore striding toward them across the beach with a frustrated frown on his face.

"What in God's good name happened to these men?" the sergeant spat. "Where were the Indians?"

The soldier turned his head and stared blankly at him. At first Willie though that the man was going to strike the sergeant. Then the wounded officer moaned again and the soldier directed his attention back to him. The soldier began to speak slowly, not looking up.

"It was in the early evening. We were searchin' along a creek off the Jupiter River when we seen a light from a fire. We landed our flat boats and went ashore and made camp. At daylight the next day we came upon an old Indian trail that led inland. We followed it and eventually came to a clearing in which were discovered a large number of horses and cows. We took this as a sign that there were savages about. We searched the immediate area and came up with nothing. We moved further up the trail and heard a noise to the front of us. Danged if two of our men stumbled upon an old Indian squaw hidin' in the trees. She appeared to be starvin' to death and very sick. Her clothes was badly rotted and torn, and her shriveled face was hard fer me to look at. I wondered how it could happen that she was here by herself. What kind of people would allow this to happen to one of their old squaws?"

The soldier paused at this and looked up at Willie and the Sergeant, shaking his head at the bad memory. He reached down by his feet and picked up a glass jar half full of water, then tipped it to this mouth and took a few swallows. He then placed the jar to the lips of the wounded officer and helped him drink. He then continued to speak, his voice softer.

"As I looked at that old woman my hatred for them savage killers grew. She didn't speak our language and seemed to be rightly terrified by our fierceness. We demanded of her the location of the village where her savage people were. She tried to tell us, but it weren't no use. We did not have any of the interpreters with us who could speak that savage tongue. Finally, after we fed her some of our rations, she seemed to understand what we wanted. She also understood what we would do if she didn't comply with us. She led us further up a different trail that led off to the southwest. It was rough goin' with several nearly impassable areas. The sand filled our shoes and the saw grass tore at our clothes. The skeeters feasted on our skin mercilessly. We walked for miles, and we soon started to wonder where the old hag was leadin' us! At about four o'clock in the afternoon, we were marching around the edge of a great cypress hammock when we heard a sound that sent chills up our spines. It was somethin' in between the cry of an animal and a woman's scream. It started out like a low growlin' noise and rose to a piercing shriek. The men were lookin' around, their heads turnin' wildly all around, for its source. Then there was this explosion of gunfire and Lt. Harrison, who was directly in front of me, spun around and fell with the impact of a ball to his head. Well, let me tell you, all hell broke loose after that. We was flat under attack. The noise that we had heard was the terrible Seminole battle cry. Lieutenant Fowler ordered us to charge the hammock and attack with all urgency. I remember thinking to myself, "Attack what?" We could not see any savages at all. They had hid themselves so well."

The soldier paused and stared off at nothing. It seemed to Willie that he did not care if anyone was listening to him. After a few long moments he continued. Willie and the sergeant were riveted to his every word as he spoke.

"We rushed forward as a group past some empty Indian campsites until we came to a shallow river. I believe that this was the *Locha-Hatchee*, because I seen it on a map back here before we left. We could see more crude shelters and women and children runnin' about on the other side. That was the part I hated the most; seeing them kids runnin' like that.

After some time we were able to push all of the savages back to the other side of this river, but when the men reached it, they refused to cross. The place we were in was thick with palmetto trees and deep water up to above our knees. The brutes were firin' on us from secure positions in the dang trees. They were beginnin' to gain the day and many men fell. The sailors just panicked and broke because they were not skilled fighters. I never seen more scared men than them fellas. Most of them had never fired the muskets that they was now carryin'. They began to cut and run wild and aimless through that swamp. It was terrible. I personally saw that doctor fella that was with us take a ball to the chest. He was so badly wounded that we had to leave him behind. Not just him, but others too. If it wasn't for that engineer man, Johnston, we'd have all been kilt. That man showed mighty courage in the face of that terrible enemy. He organized the men into some semblance of order and got us out of the worst of it so we could get back to our boats. He took seven or eight shots through his clothes and even one through his hat! We was in such a sorry state as we ran that we had to leave all of them dead and even some wounded behind. We was in such a hurry that, as the last of our boats pulled away, we nearly left Mr. Johnston alone on that beach."

At the conclusion of the soldier's story, Sergeant Moore stood up, shook his head and walked back toward the fort. Willie placed his hand on the soldiers shoulder and said, "God helped bring you men back to us. We can thank him for that."

Willie turned and walked back to the fort. As he approached the gate, he paused for a moment to contemplate the burial mound. He shook his head as he remembered the wild osprey attack and the terrible dreams that he had experienced afterward. He felt a general sense of unease after seeing Powell's men all battered and defeated. How would he have acted under similar circumstances? He wasn't sure.

"The Removal" by Dave Geister

The March to Locha- Hatchee

Later that day Willie and Josiah learned that their division had received orders to move out the next morning to Camp Lloyd to the west, where they would join forces with Eustis's forces. The boys were apprehensive and discouraged that they had to leave the amenities of Fort Pierce and its cool river breezes for the expansive, swampy, blisteringly hot scrub pine prairie that they knew so well from their original journey south. Willie was so exhausted by the previous night's terrors that he had no dreams, and was up at first light with all of the other men.

The rumor among the men was that General Jesup was very impatient to get moving and wanted to smash the

Seminoles at *Locha-Hatchee* with a decisive blow and end the war soon. He was going to ride west and then south with a force of about five-hundred mounted men as an advance party with the rest of the great army following at a slower pace. The first units to depart Fort Pierce were the General's men and Harney's Second Dragoons along with the mounted Alabama and Tennessee Volunteers under Major Lauderdale. The artillery force, including Willie and Josiah, would follow with their cannons, pack mules and Dearborn wagons.

The weather the first day was clear and the terrain wet around the hammocks as they slogged west through sawgrass about three feet high and ankle deep water. The sun was beating down on the men and there was no cover in sight for miles. As the boys walked side by side making their slow progress, Josiah talked constantly. Willie was lost in thought and hypnotically watched the feet and back of the soldier marching in front of him. He was still thinking of the terrible nightmare of the Indian ghost lady. He could feel the weight of the sack containing the bones bouncing on his side.

Josiah grew bored and continued to babble incessantly.

"I reckon we'll kill us some savages before this campaign is up," he said. "I am gonna be at my most fierce."

Willie did not answer.

Josiah continued. "I can't believe that this war will continue much longer after they see the size of this force. We should be goin' home in a month."

Willie turned his head and looked at his friend.

"If we don't move faster than we are, we won't see the savages for a month." he said.

"Josiah, can I ask you a question?"

Josiah looked back at Willie, glad that his friend had decided to talk.

"Yes, sure, go ahead."

"Do you believe in spirits, you know, haints?"

"You mean like, ghosts?"

"Yes, I guess that's what you would call it."

Josiah paused at this for a moment as if contemplating the question and admired a red-shouldered hawk that flew in lazy circles in the sky to the north. After a few seconds he spoke.

"I reckon there could be spirits, Willie. I heard that the leader of the Seminole savages might be a spirit. The officers call him "Sam Jones", but his real name is Arpeeka or something. He supposedly has four souls, and can't be hit by bullets. I'd have to see that to believe it, though. Why are you askin' me that, Willie?"

"I don't know, Josiah. I'm just askin."

Willie noticed that the morale of the men was high that morning with thoughts of retribution on their minds. The Volunteers were laughing and joking with each other and singing the Garryowen song as they marched. They were making the officers and many soldiers angry by periodically shooting their weapons at any animals that moved in the underbrush of the hammocks as they passed by. About midday the army paused for a rest in a slightly raised fairly dry area. There were words between a burly soldier and a large rough looking volunteer, and a fight erupted. The two men pounded each other and rolled about in the swamp mud as a crowd formed around them. The action was soon interrupted by the scream of an officer, and the men soon resumed their wet slog westward.

Willie knew, as almost all of the men did, of the tension between the volunteers and the regular soldiers. The soldiers had the discipline that the army provided and were disdainful of the lax regulations and lack of military training of the Tennessee volunteers. This was an unruly mob of men whose members behaved, in Willie's opinion, in a most un-military fashion. They drank whiskey at night from small flasks that they had brought with them, and stayed up late laughing and carousing around their campfires like they were on some sort of hunting excursion. Many of the soldiers used the term "rascals" when they referred to these "farmers" from Tennessee and Alabama. There were more than a few heated discussions and fisticuffs when the officers weren't looking. During the march the volunteers maintained their own line to the left and did not mix with the soldiers.

They covered about fifteen miles through the swamp before they made camp on a large raised hammock covered with trees. Willie and Josiah found a dry area and pitched the tent. They were so tired that they didn't even light a fire. They ate their dry rations and fell asleep right away. Willie dreamed that he was being chased through a large black emptiness by an unseen evil. It was a mere inches from catching him as he ran with the same aching slowness that he had experienced in his previous nightmare. He woke abruptly in the dark of night, his body again drenched in sweat. He looked over at the cloth bag that held the bones from the mound and stared at it, his fear rising. He could have sworn that it had taken on an almost imperceptible but very eerie white glow. He rolled over on his side and shook with fright, and could not sleep the rest of the night.

The next day, as the army approached Camp Lloyd, the landscape grew even more inhospitable. The ground became even more wet and deep and the cypress knees proved even more hazardous, especially for the horses. Willie watched as a mounted dragoon was thrown into the swamp when his horse staggered and fell forward. The animal had twisted and broken its leg on a cypress knee and had to be shot.

The men plodded along mile after mile through the water, and Willie worried that his shoes would never again be dry. The foot deep water made it harder to walk and added to his exhaustion. He and Josiah slogged on and, as the long hours passed, wondered if they would ever get to the camp. Eventually they did, but there was not much relief in what they found there. Camp Lloyd was a flat, desolate place constructed of palmetto logs on a high cleared hammock by Colonel Zachary Taylor's men just before the battle at *O-ke-cho-bee*. There were many soldiers already there, these being

General Eustis's men. They were a rough looking lot, having just made a march of two hundred miles through the same bad terrain that Willie and Josiah had just encountered. Their uniforms were faded and torn and their faces heavily bearded. Some of them wore uniforms fashioned from sacks or rawhide leather that they had acquired on the march from the north. Eustis himself was a gruff man with a loud voice and a no-nonsense air about him. The boys intended to stay clear of these men as much as they could, so they set camp and spent one night just outside of the picket walls of Camp Lloyd. Willie was so exhausted that he saw no Indian ghosts this night.

They were awoken early by the bleating sound of reveille. The entire force now numbered between fifteen and sixteen hundred men. General Jesup and his five-hundred strong mounted advance force had ridden out in the near darkness two hours earlier, leaving the rest of the army to follow at the slower pace. The mules were packed, the artillery prepared, and the men fed their meager rations. The army started off toward the great *Al-pa-ti-o-kie* swamp like a great serpentine beast. Willie and Josiah were happy to be heading south, but wary and fearful of what lay waiting ahead. The weather had held, but it was very hot and uncomfortable with the ground still deep with water in between the hammocks.

"I'll tell ya, Willie, I can't wait to git into some fightin," Josiah said with what Willie thought of as false bravado. Willie knew that his friend was nervous, anxious, and half exhausted.

"I'm sure that you'll show 'em." Willie said.

Josiah was quiet for a while as they walked as if deep in thought. Presently, he spoke again.

"Willie, do you ever get scared?"

"Well, I reckon I do, Josiah."

"Can I make a confession to you? You promise not to laugh?"

Willie gave his friend a sideways look.

"What is it?" he asked.

"I get scared sometimes. I hear the stories of these savages and I get so worked up that I can't stop thinkin' 'bout it."

"Josiah, I think every man gets scared sometimes. The way I look at it is that when you have something to do, you do it. You don't think about it too much, you just do what you got to do, you know? If you think about somethin' too much it starts to eat you up inside. Just keep thinkin' bout the men that the savages killed and how we are goin' to make it right."

Josiah was quiet after this. The boys set about walking in stony silence.

Willie thought of the strange dreams that he had been having. He had started to convince himself that he was being haunted by spirits that wanted to kill him. He knew that he was not heeding the advice that he had just given to his friend. He could not stop thinking of the strange maiden apparition that he had seen. She seemed so sad and terrible. He remembered that the spirit had asked him why he had taken the bones from the mound. It occurred to him then that he might be able to end this by getting rid of them. He could throw the damn things into the swamp right now. It might be just as easy as that. He pondered this thought for a while as he trudged along with the others through the wet, endless terrain.

173

After a time, his thoughts took a different tack. Why was he afraid of this stupid dream, anyway? He was a soldier, for god's sake. He had found the bones and the necklace himself, and he was going to keep them as souvenirs of this godforsaken place and this war. He was going to take them back to Tennessee.

The army walked in three large columns moving across the rough wet terrain of the swampy Florida everglades. The left column was made up of the remainder of Twigg's and Harney's mounted dragoons that hadn't gone ahead with Jesup's advance force. The horses suffered greatly because of the deep water, twisting roots, and jutting cypress knees. They frequently fell and became mired and stuck, so the mounted soldiers had to spend a large amount of their time in water up to their knees pulling the reluctant beasts along. The poor animals often suffered broken legs and had to be shot. They were then promptly skinned and butchered to feed the relentless hunger of the men.

The center column was made up of the pack mules and artillery. The mules suffered almost as much as the horses as they struggled to haul the dis-assembled six pound howitzers on their backs and pull the lurching Dearborn wagons along through the swampy palmetto scrub.

The right column was made up of the remaining Tennessee and Alabama Volunteers, many of whom were not mounted and thus forced to trudge along on foot. They argued and complained incessantly throughout the long days of marching. Many of the men's shoes simply gave out due to the miserable conditions leaving a large number of them barefoot. They had to be very careful about keeping their weapons and powder dry.

Late in the afternoon one of the men near Willie and Josiah let out a terrified scream and jumped to the side, falling into the water with a splash. Willie saw a thick black snake let go of his leg with a violent jerk of its triangular head and slither away into the saw grass. The man grabbed his leg and howled in pain as the venom started to eat away at the muscle. Three soldiers came to his aid and helped him to his feet as he screamed and cussed violently. Several of the men were unfortunate enough to have encountered attacks like this from water moccasins and rattlesnakes hiding in the roots of the trees in the hammocks. These poor men ended up at the rear of the company limping along and eventually dying, their bodies left to rot in the glaring sun.

The army stopped for the night at small clearing next to a very large hammock that afforded slightly higher ground than the rest of the terrain. The men were miserably tired and hungry from the long terrible march. The main body of the army had caught up with Jesup and the Second Dragoons because they had encountered a fairly good sized river and had to wait until Lt. Robert Anderson's Third Artillery Regiment of construction men could build a rough bridge across it. These men would work all through the night, enduring mosquito bites and darkness to perform this arduous task.

Willie and Josiah pitched their tent on a small dry spot in between some trees. The exhausted boys sat around their fire eating their meager rations of hardtack and sardines. Josiah was leaning back in a crook between two turkey oak trees. He had his split, broken shoes off and was massaging his swollen feet, periodically slapping at the mosquitoes that landed on his bare skin.

"Willie, you ever miss home?" Josiah asked as he stared into the flames. The boy's faces were orange in the firelight and the smell of burning wood filled their nostrils.

"Hell yeah, I'd kill for one of Susan's apple pies right about now," Willies answered in a low voice.

"I'm not sure how much more my feet will take, Willie. I never thought it would get this bad. I never would have joined this damn army if I knew this was gonna happen."

"Don't you worry, Josiah, I'll look after ya. Remember when we left home to join up? Yer momma was so mad at us, so I promised her I would take care of you."

His friend didn't answer. Willie looked at him and saw that he had fallen asleep against the tree. He gazed at Josiah's face and noticed how innocent the boy looked. He reflected on their shared childhood experiences and smiled as he remembered all of the times that they had gotten into trouble together as they were growing up back home. His thoughts changed to concern as he realized that he would never forgive himself if anything happened to Josiah. He knew what he had to do.

Silver Moon- Jackie Brice

Ghost Hammock

Willie crawled into the tent on his hands and knees and located the cloth bag that contained the skull and the necklace. He got up and walked away from their fire toward a large clearing just west of the camp. The moon was full and the features of the landscape were starkly visible in the azure-blue of night. Willie saw the white of the countless canvas tents reflected in the moonlight and heard the nickering of horses fixed to the many rope lines that had been run from tree to tree across the edge of the clearing. It was much cooler than during the day and he enjoyed the breeze across his skin. He could see the orange glow of the many fires that were still burning as he made his way out toward the trees away from camp. He didn't know why, but he felt compelled to separate himself from the others and walk further and further into the swampy landscape.

He soon came to the edge of a large hammock that was densely covered in live oak, poison ivy, and palmetto trees. He peered into its denseness, not quite sure what it was that he was looking for. He heard a sound from deep inside it and felt his heart leap with fear. He heard a sound; a low moan that seemed almost like a woman's crying. Was it her? Was it the Indian Spirit? He pulled up the cloth bag and reached his hand inside of it, gripping the skull. He looked back into the hammock and began to shout in a hoarse whisper.

"Hey, I know you're there! I know what you want!"

He stopped to listen, but heard nothing.

"Hey! I want you to leave me alone! I brought what you wanted!" he shouted.

He pulled the skull out of the bag, drew back his arm, and hurled it into the hammock. He heard it bounce off a tree and land on the ground with a crunching sound. He paused again and listened for a response.

He nearly jumped out of his skin when there was another sound to his rear.

"Ohhh!"

The noise came from directly behind him, no more than three feet away. He whirled around and found himself staring face to face with a horrifying sight. It was a man, but not a man. It glowed with a pale shimmer that radiated out at least a foot and a half all the way around it. It was an apparition that he could see straight through, but its features were distinct and clear. It stared at him with hollow, black circles where the eyes should have been. Willie let out a small cry and stepped backward, tripping over a root and falling down on his back into the wetness of the ground. He looked up at the creature in disbelief and shock as it hovered above him. He saw that it was dressed in disheveled and torn military attire, and that there were two terrible wounds on its body. They were visible through shredded voids in the cloth of the uniform and were not bleeding, but appeared to be open and black jagged holes that hung with flaps of torn and loose flesh. One of the wounds was on its chest and the other exactly like it lower on the right side of its abdomen. The specter's mouth was twisted in a grimacing half-smile that seemed almost mocking in appearance. In spite of his terror, a dark realization came to him. He recognized this spirit. It was that doctor from Powell's expedition! The soldier on the beach had told him that the man was killed by the savages!

In an attempt to escape from its horrible gaze, Willie began to crab-walk backward away from the thing until he ran into a tree and could go no further. The spirit did not move toward him, but stayed where it was and held its chilling stare. It seemed to pulsate with an unnatural energy that it seemed to be barely able to contain. Willie found himself speechless and literally paralyzed with fear. The thing did not move for a few moments as it appeared to float a few inches above the wet ground in front of him. Then, almost imperceptibly, it bowed toward him in a mock greeting. Willie heard a soft sound, like a whisper, that seemed to fill his head. He realized that the terrible phantom was talking to him.

"Willie, you have a destiny."

He stared blankly at the spirit, as if trying to comprehend what he was hearing. The voice continued.

"You will help us to protect the old ones, Willie."

The horrible mouth held that awful mocking smile, not moving at all.

"We will do this together."

Willie began to look wildly from side to side, searching for an escape. The spirit went silent and just hovered there, its sardonic gaze unwavering.

Willie regained a small amount of his composure. He rolled to his right, sprang to his feet, and ran toward the south edge of the dark hammock. His clothes caught on some branches and he stumbled and tripped over a log, landing roughly on the ground. He scrambled back to his feet, and as he did he heard laughter behind him. He burst out onto the flat terrain of the saw grass plain and ran as fast as he could. The moon shone brightly and the cool breeze blew over his sweat covered body. He felt weak from fear and was trembling with adrenaline. He ran back to his tent, crept inside quietly, and buried his head under his blanket.

A few hours later Willie opened his eyes. The sky held the semi-darkness of very early morning. He could hear the sounds of the men moving about outside, and he smelled the smoke of the morning campfires. He looked over at Josiah's side of the tent and saw that his friend was still sleeping. He sat up and rubbed his face with his hands to wake up. The memory of the events of the night before suddenly came to him, and he shook his head back and forth to try and rid himself of the images. He pinched the bridge of his nose to try and relieve some pressure as the tell-tale signs of an approaching headache became evident. Had it all been another one of his nightmares?

He heard a sound from the dirt floor at the right side of the tent opening and caught a glimpse of some movement. He recognized the fluid motion of it and called to his friend in a dry, rasping whisper.

"Josiah! Wake your ass up! Now!"

He saw a stir of motion as his friend nodded to wakefulness.

"What the hell, Willie?"

"Don't move, but there's a big ole' cottonmouth right next to you!"

"Oh Jeesus Willie! What do I do now?"

"Relax and don't make no sudden moves," he told Josiah in a sharp whisper.

He could see the snake now. It was curled up and looking straight at him. Its tongue darted out and its emerald eyes glared at him with reptilian indifference. It was very thick and imposing. Willie very slowly reached to his side for his rifle. He knew that if he provoked it, it would come at him. He had seen these snakes in action many times during his time in Florida. He slowly grabbed the weapon by the barrel and pulled it to him. He had no intention of trying to shoot the snake, but had quickly formed another plan. He slowly raised his weapon to his side, the stock facing the serpent.

"Willie, where is it?" Josiah whined. The snake turned its attention toward him.

"Shut up, Josiah. I am going to try somethin', but you need to keep real quiet."

Willie waited a moment, not moving. Then, with a quick thrusting motion, he rammed the stock of his rifle under the bulk of the snakes coiled body, at the same time lifting it up. It hissed at him and attempted to gather for a strike, but it did not have time. In a scooping motion, Willie shoveled it out the tent flap door and into the morning. The snake slithered off through the grass.

"What happened, Willie, is it gone?" Josiah asked, his voice quavering.

Willie didn't speak for a moment. He shook his head slowly and stared out into the dim light of the morning.

"Josiah, I'm startin' to miss home real bad," he said resignedly.

2nd Dragoons- Army- Navy Chronicles

The Battle of Locha-Hatchee

The boys emerged from their tent carrying their muskets and were surprised by an unexpected sight.

"Indians!" Josiah exclaimed.

Willie saw that there were, indeed, a large company of Indians standing around in close proximity to their tent. He saw that they were armed to the teeth and very intimidating in appearance. They were dressed in colorful shirts and buckskin, and were performing various tasks such as tending to their mounts, cleaning weapons, squatting around small fires, and eating. He stared at them in astonishment, and they looked back at him with almost insolent silence. He heard a voice to his left, a high pitched irritating harangue.

"Relax, there, soldier! These boys ain't Seminole savages. These are Delaware's from the north who come into camp durin' the night. They's fightin' with us!"

He recognized the source of the voice as Ambrose Hill, a junior officer he had known for a while and didn't particularly like. Hill was leaning back against a live oak tree and laughing.

"You act like you seen a ghost, McCracken! You and your girl there better go get some grub soon, we'll be movin' out di-rectly!"

"Watch who yer callin' a girl, there!" Josiah called back angrily. He started to move toward Hill, so Willie grabbed him by his tunic and pulled him back. He shot Hill an angry glance and walked off toward the wagons, pulling Josiah along behind him.

The march to the south was soon underway again. The army made their way across the river on the roughly hewn bridge and continued the monotonous slog through the pine flats and cypress swamps. The soldiers soon found themselves wading through waist deep water. Many had trouble finding their footing and stumbled along as best they could. Some had lost their shoes in the deep muck and were now barefoot and suffering greatly. Their bearded and haggard faces held expressions of dogged, exhausted determination as they continued their slow progress. The general mood of the men was not pleasant and morale had suffered among the ranks.

As Willie made his way through the sawgrass, he could not stop thinking about the terrible nightmares that were haunting him. What had the vision of the doctor's spirit meant? Was it trying to send a message of some sort? What would cause terrible dreams like this? Josiah was complaining about his sore feet for what Willie thought was the hundredth time when they received the news from the advance scouts: The Seminoles were about four miles ahead.

A tight anticipation replaced the foul mood of the men. The majority of them seemed ready to unleash a mighty anger on their unseen enemy. They had something else to preoccupy their minds now besides the miserable conditions. Willie felt both a thrill and a sense of dread as he tried to pick up his pace. As the army moved further south, the terrain seemed to get even rougher. They heard firing in the distance, and could soon see a giant hammock of trees across the long expanse of a wet sawgrass slew. With a sinking feeling, Willie realized that the Seminoles had chosen this spot for a reason. The shooting grew more intense, and he could see poofs of white smoke emanating from the high trees of the hammock. He watched as the mounted dragoons tried to approach it with a direct assault, only to have their horses stop abruptly and refuse to continue as the water reached the tops of the men's saddles. The reality of the situation became evident to him when he saw a man, an officer, take a ball to the chest and flip back off his horse into the wet sawgrass. The remaining dragoons were forced to make the agonizingly slow maneuver of turning back and pulling their tired and suffering mounts back out of range. They then bravely charged into the wet slew on foot with the infantry and artillery.

"Josiah, you stay close to me, ok? I need you to do that!" he shouted at his friend.

Josiah looked at him and shook his head, his glazed eyes betraying the fear that was gripping him.

"You need to keep your rifle up out of the water, you hear? If you get your powder wet you're dead!"

"Ok, Willie," his friend answered as they made their way toward the trees.

As they moved forward, closer to the main section of fighting, Willie could see more smoke from the Seminole gunfire rising from high in the trees. He realized that their sharpshooters had positioned themselves up there where they would have clear aim at the approaching soldiers. He watched the rest of the artillery men struggle to drag the six pound howitzer cannons through the water of the slew up into range, where they could commence firing into the impenetrable hammock. He could see the Tennessee Volunteers on the left making their way to the northwest side of the trees. He felt the heat and fearful excitement of the battle as he got closer to the enemies entrenched position. To his right he saw that several soldiers had set up the iron tubes and rough "A" frame supports of the Congreve rockets. They had a flintlock style igniting systems and were launched by pulling a long cord from a short distance away. He heard the screams of these rockets as they made their twisting, inaccurate trajectory of destruction through the impenetrable foliage of the hammock.

The enemy was so well concealed that the majority of the soldiers had not yet laid eyes on one of them, so the first of them to make their way into the hammock shot wildly at anything that moved. After a while, the intense barrage from the musket fire, cannons, and rockets succeeded in pushing the Seminole warriors back to a retreating position, but the screams of the wounded and general confusion of battle had not ceased.

Willie finally got to the edge of the trees. There was so much going on around him that he had not thought to fire his musket even once. He looked around wildly for Josiah, but could not locate him. He stumbled, and was horrified to see that what he had tripped over was the sprawled body of a Seminole warrior that had no head, just a bloody stump where it used to be. He began to run, darting around cabbage palm and pine trees as he heard the whining of balls flying over his head. Some of them ricocheted off trees and threw splinters of wood that sprayed him as he ran. He saw others running alongside him through the smoke that now filled the thicket, but he still did not see Josiah. He looked ahead and saw many large cypress trees on a river bank in the distance. He felt a wave of fear so acute that he felt lightheaded and thought he may pass out. He heard an officer screaming to hit the river fast and hard. He held his rifle high and made for that bank. When he reached it, he was running too fast and tripped over some roots, falling head over heels down the bank and into the warm water of the *Locha-Hatchee*. He found himself completely submerged and floundering around in the water, waving his arms wildly.

His head broke the surface and his feet found purchase on the bottom. He cursed himself loudly and realized that the water was only about four feet deep. Luckily, he had dropped his rifle on the bank before his clumsy fall into the water. Other soldiers were there moving past him, clambering through the river, holding their weapons above their heads. He scrambled back to the bank and snatched up his weapon, quickly checking that it was not broken. As he was doing this, he heard a great commotion in the bushes near him. He looked up into the baleful face of a horse. His eyes moved upward and into the intense, battle wild eyes of Colonel Harney of the Dragoons. Harney looked down at him, a look of disgust and anger on his bearded face, and barked an order. At first Willie didn't understand it, but as his mind focused the man's instructions became clear.

"Soldier! Quit playing with that weapon and look down there to the south in them trees down yonder! We need to find any savages that might be hiding there!

"Yes sir!" Willie answered.

With that, Harney turned his horse and rode fast down the edge of the river to the south, his horse's hooves throwing up mud clumps as it ran.

He started to get that light-headed feeling again and had to sit down. He put his face in his hands. What was wrong with him? He felt sick and thought he was going to vomit. He didn't know how much time passed; maybe minutes, maybe hours. He could not move. After a time, he heard someone behind him call his name.

"Willie! You're alive!"

"Josiah!" Willie answered. He started to get up, but felt the weakness come on him again.

Josiah sat down next to him on the bank. He was filthy, as if he had been rolling in the mud, but his eyes gleamed with excitement.

"What in hell are you doin' here? The fightin's off to the north!" Josiah exclaimed.

"Gall darn, it, Josiah! I know where the fightin' is! I didn't think they was shootin' turkeys over there!"

There was an awkward silence, and then his demeanor softened a bit as he realized how glad he was to see his friend safe and unharmed.

"I fell down the bank," he said sheepishly, "I damn near broke my neck."

Josiah ignored what he had said and began talking in an eager, petulant manner.

"I went all the way to the north part of the river where the savages were shootin' across the river. Them Tennessee Volunteers under ole Major Lauderdale was ordered to advance by Jesup hisself. But, you know, Willie, they wouldn't move, not even for Jesup. He was mad as a stoked hornet, Willie, you should've seen it! I seen the ole man run out in the hottest part of the firin' himself. I couldn't believe it, Willie. He was hollerin' and waving his pistol, tryin' to get them fellers to move across that part of the river where it was shallow. He's carryin' on like that and one of them Seminole savages lets loose with a ball that could've have took his head clean off, but it wasn't straight, you know? It hits him in the face with a glancing blow and knocks his glasses off his face. I tell ya, Willie, I ain't never seen nothin'like that. After this, he walks right up to Major Lauderdale on his horse, his face bleedin', and points his pistol right at him and says sumthin' like, "If you don't git these men across that river, I'll blow yer head right off, right here!"

Willie was only half listening. He was feeling angry as he realized that he had not participated in the fighting at all. He had spent the whole fight here on this bank like a woman, crying and puking. He stood up and looked down the river to the south.

"I can't stand here jabberin' with you, Josiah. Colonel Harney himself commissioned me to find savages that may be hidin' in this part of the river. I'll see you later back at camp."

With that, he strode off down the riverbank to the south. Josiah angrily watched as Willie walked away, then got up, climbed the river bank, and ran off to the north where the shooting continued in the distance. Willie could hear that the intense firing was starting to slow down and knew that the main fighting had moved off toward the northeast. He was still very angry and frustrated. Looking ahead, he saw movement in some palmettos on the west side of the river. He caught a glimpse of a figure moving in front of him behind some wide, concealing leaves. He heard something familiar and completely out of place. It sounded like a child crying; an infant! He carefully advanced and pushed the leaves aside with barrel of his musket. He could not believe what he saw. It was a Seminole squaw, very young, probably still in her teens trying to hide in the waist deep water. There were tears streaming down her face. In her hands was a bundle in a blanket that she was holding under the water. A terrible realization came over Willie and he felt his heart nearly stop. She was holding her crying baby under the surface of the water to avoid detection.

Willie was stunned. He did not know what to do. He threw his arms out toward the girl and pulled the baby up out of the water. It coughed and sputtered, but seemed to be alive. His mind was immediately filled with thoughts of his own children back in Tennessee, safe on the farm. All of a sudden he experienced a whole new wave of emotion. He felt his eyes burst with tears as the realization came to him that this whole ridiculous war was a terrible waste and very, very wrong. He felt his arms rise to embrace the girl and her baby. The terrified girl backed away from him and turned her head toward the opposite bank.

He spun his head to where she looked and saw the dark face of a black Seminole warrior wearing a wide, red turban. The man was drawing a bead on him with his long rifle, a sneer on his mouth and a look of hatred in his dark eyes. Willie, in a blind panic, instinctively brought his rifle up one-handed, at the same time pulling the trigger. It was a random, un-aimed shot, and both weapons went off almost simultaneously. Willie felt the impact of the ball in his head in an explosion of light, and he felt himself falling to the water. The last thing he saw were the tear filled eyes of the young girl as she watched him. His last thoughts were of his wife and children as the warm water of the *Locha-Hatchee* closed over his head. Then there was no more pain in his feet, no more hunger, no more worry, no more nightmares.

Willie felt himself slip into the water, his body becoming part of it. He felt the animals in the forest, the trees, the air, everything. He felt his spirit searching for something. He moved as if unencumbered by any human restraints. He sensed the Indian Woman Spirit near him, now not malevolent, but caring. He saw her then, her hands outstretched, welcoming him. He felt his body changing; his vision sharpening, his muscles growing stronger, his breath growing fast. He looked down, and his hands were paws, and his arms were covered with fur. He quickly darted through the forest; his hunger growing with every stride. He had become a quick, elusive and cunning bobcat.

HAUNTED RIVER TALES

CHAPTER 4

LEVI

Dudley Farmhouse- Marion W. Hylton

WEST JUPITER, 1928

Levi drove the wagon into the yard between the small clapboard farmhouse and the barn. He reined the mules to a stop, got down from the wagon, and untied them. He stretched his tired arms out wide and yawned, then unlatched and pulled the two tall, roughly hewn doors open. He led the two animals into the barn and into their individual stalls for feeding. He walked back outside and reached into the wagon, pulling the whiskey jug from under the seat. Tugging the cork out with a "thuk" sound, he raised the jug to his lips, allowing an ample amount of the bitter moonshine liquor into his mouth.

"Honeydew vine water!" he exclaimed as he swiped his sleeve across his lips.

He replaced the cork, giving it a light smack with the palm of his hand to secure it. Slipping his finger through the round carrying handle, he walked out of the barn, the jug swinging at his side. He closed the doors behind him and lowered the wrought iron latch.

Levi was a stout, handsome man; fairly short, about five-foot-five inches tall. He carried a little more weight than he should have, mostly due to the love of his wife Martha's apple pies. He was forty-three years to Martha's thirty, and his blond hair had gone mostly gray. The lower half of his face was covered by a full beard that had, over the years, turned white. The tobacco that he chewed on all day long constantly puffed out his mouth at the lower lip. The worn overalls and flannel shirt that he wore all the time, even on Sunday, seemed like a part of his skin. He wore tall leather boots that came up to his knees for prevention of snakebites from the diamondback rattlers or water moccasins that he encountered frequently in his work in the groves or near the river. Having learned many years ago what the Florida sun could do to a fair skinned man in a day, he wore a wide brimmed cotton hat to cover his head and the pale skin of his neck.

His wide smile and good humor gained him many friends among the employees here in the groves and in Jupiter to the east. He was musically talented and often played an old banjo that he had brought with him from Tennessee years earlier. The children cackled with delight as he broke out into song, telling them the story of the "Battle of New Orleans" or some other musical tale. He knew the words to many old songs and was often the center of entertainment at the Saturday night square dances that were held at the church in town once a month.

His friend and co-worker, Enos, lived with the other black employees and their families on the other side of the Loxahatchee River. Even though the man's skin color was different than his, Levi considered him to be his closest friend, and he loved working with him. Enos had unstoppable energy and could work all day in the scorching sun without a break. Tall and thin, but possessing great hidden physical strength, he was about the same age as Levi, forty, but looked younger. When he worked in the groves he wore a fairly ragged shirt and denim overalls that were faded in very rough shape. The features of his unshaven face glistened with sweat on his almost blue, black skin. On his head was a wide brimmed, cotton hat that had a large permanent sweat stain around the brim. His large, expressive eyes and broad mouth seemed to hold a serious expression most of the time. He was deeply religious and not afraid to speak his mind about his beliefs.

Levi smiled to himself as he thought of how the man could work circles around him.

"Enos, I'm, older, fatter, and lazier than you. And the funny thing is I'm damn proud of it."

"Yes, Levi, I can't figure for the life of me why they keep you around."

"That's easy, Enos. I'm a worldly man, and that's a trait that's hard to come by, let me tell ya."

This often got the desired sardonic look from Enos that Levi wanted. The two men generally liked and respected one another and spent the day throwing barbs at each other and arguing about everything from politics to women. It really helped to pass the long workdays in the Florida sun, and they both appreciated each other's company.

He had been thinking a lot lately about his little family out here in the groves and his situation in general. He knew that it was due to his stubborn insistence that they move out here to live by the river that they had so little to show after these years of work.

That was going to soon change, he thought.

His wife, Martha, had always supported his decisions completely, and he knew that she would follow him anywhere. But where was he leading her? He had first heard of the Jupiter area as a child when he learned that his great grandfather, Willie McCracken, had been killed down here somewhere during the Second Seminole War about ninety years earlier. He had read some of the man's letters to his grandmother about the land down here: how beautiful it was, how good the fishing was, how much open land there was, things like that. Levi had always wanted to come here. It was only after he had packed up Martha and their few belongings and actually made the trip from Tennessee that the reality of life in Southeast Florida had kicked in. It was a hard life indeed. The soil was bad, it was very hot and humid most of the time, and the mosquitoes were terrible in the summer months. He had been lucky to get this job here at the groves, and he intended to keep it. The grove owners had given him his own plot of land and let him build his little castle on it. Martha had adapted quickly to the rigorous frontier lifestyle and had rolled up her sleeves to help Levi build a life. Over the years she had given him three healthy fine children in between the never-ending chores and responsibilities of farm life. They were happy, but Levi knew that he was soon going to give Martha and his children much more.

Walking to the woodpile a few feet from the side of the house, Levi bent down and, with one hand, picked up a rough chunk of firewood and carried it and his jug across the yard. He stepped up onto the crooked porch and walked past the old wooden rocker toward the front door. Before he entered, he bent and set the whiskey jug down. He then walked into the cabin, pulling the door closed behind him. He strode across the floor and placed the logs by the fireplace.

"Home safe!" he cried, as was his nightly custom.

"Papa! Papa! Come play with us!" screamed the twin girls, Elly and Carleen, almost in unison as they ran to him.

205

He smiled and dropped to his knees, opening his arms as they ran across the plank floor into his embrace.

"How's m'girls! I missed ya while I was workin'!"

He caught them both in a bear hug and picked them both up off the floor a few inches, smothering them with kisses. They giggled and kicked their bare feet in the air.

"Levi McCracken!" his wife said in a stern voice, "You don't have time to be fussin' with them girls. You'd best be gittin' ready for supper!"

"Aww, Ma, you know I ain't seen my favorite girls all day and I missed 'em mightily!" he said in a playful voice, "I also missed somebody else!"

With that, he walked to Martha and gathered her in a big embrace, kissing her on the face, as the children howled with laughter.

"Levi, you're incorrigible! Not in front of the children!" she scolded him, barely containing her laughter.

Her expression changed to mock concern and she playfully socked him on the chest with her fist.

"I smell that awful moonshine on you!"

Martha loved this part of the day. Levi's coming home from work was a major event in their little family. She loved him more than anything on earth, and she had followed him to this godforsaken end of it. She knew that he was a hard worker and had only the best intentions for their family. She knew that he drank too much, but he was a man and was entitled to his pleasure as long as it didn't interfere with the family too much. She had left her family behind in Tennessee to come south with him, and she was going to make the best of it if it killed her. The children idolized him. As simple and hard as it was, Martha loved her life here with Levi. She smiled and watched him swing little Elly around by her arms as the girl laughed so hard that she nearly choked.

The family ate their supper together and sat around the fireplace talking for an hour or so before the children went to bed up in the loft. When they could hear the children's even breathing, Levi and Martha talked of more serious matters.

"Levi, when are you going to get the money you deserve? The children need new clothes and shoes. You work so hard."

"I know, sweetie, I know. God provides for us, and we need to appreciate what we got."

Martha snorted a bit at that. "Huh. You could do better, Levi. You could at least have a truck to haul the oranges with. You do the work of two men out there, all day in the sun."

"Martha, you know that I am tryin' to save money right now. Besides, I like workin' with the wagon. It's quieter out there. Old Charley Jackson in Jupiter has an automobile, and its nothin' but trouble; always breakin' down."

He paused for a moment and looked into his wife's eyes, noticing how tired they looked.

"Someday I'm gonna give you everything you deserve, and more. Just give me a chance."

Her worried expression broke and she kissed him tenderly. She then went to the bedroom, softly closing the door behind her. Levi watched her go, then got up from his chair and walked to the fireplace. He got down on his knees in front of the dying fire and reached with both hands to a large stone on the left side of the hearth. He worked it back and forth, and it soon popped out. He reached into the space and pulled out an old, dirty mason jar. Unscrewing the lid, he pulled out a fat roll of paper money with a string wrapped around it. He pulled the string loose and unrolled the bills. He counted it; two, three, four; peeling the bills away one at a time. He stopped at two thousand dollars.

"Thank you Lord, for Mr. Ashley's moonshine!" he said.

Royal Poinciana- Jackie Brice

4 YEARS EARLIER

JULY, 1924

Levi had gone out hog hunting in the area north of the groves. It was a beautiful, but hot, July afternoon, and he wasn't having much luck. He wandered down an old Indian trail on the east side of the Loxahatchee, his shotgun leaning on his shoulder. He admired the beauty of the pine scrub forest and loved to get out by himself and escape into his thoughts. He had grown up in the mountainous terrain of Eastern Tennessee, and had spent his youth wandering its hills and valleys. Most northerners thought that South Florida was a swampy wasteland, but he knew different. He adored the solitude and threatening nature of the Florida wilderness. He appreciated the huge live oak and towering cypress trees; their branches dripping with sphagnum moss that billowed and swayed gently in the wind. He liked the animals of the forest; the panther, bears, otters, alligators, and even the snakes. He enjoyed the taste of rattlesnake and turtle meat when it was prepared properly. He loved to fish in his canoe, and had traveled miles up and down the river. He had caught many a good size bass in the river right here on grove property.

Near a bend in the trail he stopped. He had heard something in the distance back in the trees that sounded like an automobile driving up the access road a little to the east of him. He remembered that there was a small building in the woods a short distance to the northeast off of the grove property, so he made his way toward it to see what was going on. He had always wondered what the building was for, but he liked to mind his own business, so he never inquired about it. Keeping track of things for the groves owners was his job, and he would promptly report any funny business going on out here to them. He walked through the woods, avoiding the road, to maintain the element of surprise. The building was a little ways east of the river in a small clearing. He heard voices talking in hushed whispers.

"Who's there?" he shouted. The voices went silent.

He strode forward and emerged from the trees into the clearing. What he saw nearly made him fall over in a dead faint. There were four men in white shirts and suspenders, and two of them had hand-held revolvers trained on him. Levi took a step backward and threw his hands up, his left one holding his shotgun. He saw the rear of a Ford Model "T" Sedan parked alongside the building. The rear window glass was shattered and the black metal around it was pocked with several round paint chipped holes.

"Relax, there, friend and drop that blunderbuss yer sportin'." a calm, deep voice said.

"Whoa, now! I don't want no trouble, I'm just out hunting hogs!" he sputtered and carefully lowered his shotgun to the ground.

"Easy boys. He's harmless. He's one of them grove men. I've seen him around."

An imposing, handsome man with a shock of black hair and an eye patch over one eye walked up to Levi, gave him a broad smile, and put his arm around his shoulder.

"Hi friend. We don't want no trouble here. We got in a little scrape down south a piece and come by here for a rest, of sorts. Name's John, what's yers?" he put his hand out and gripped Levi's. His voice was even and calm, almost soothingly friendly.

"Levi McCracken, sir. I don't want no trouble either. Got a family and a job over there and want to see 'em agin fer dinner tonight," he said in a voice that quavered more than he wanted.

All of the men laughed at this.

As he looked around at the faces of the men, it slowly dawned on Levi who they were.

"I know you fellers. Yer the Ashley's, aint ya?" he asked in the same shaky voice. "Y'all ain't gonna kill me, are ya?"

Again, the men cackled. Levi gulped as he looked at a young man sitting on a stump gripping his hand in a bloody rag, a grimace of pain on his face.

"No, friend. We ain't gonna kill ya. We ain't in the killin' business. We prefer to make friends with the local gentry," the man with the eye patch said. Levi figured that he must be the gang's infamous leader, John Ashley.

This was the infamous Ashley gang. It made sense to him because there had been a recent bank robbery down south in Pompano. He looked around at each face and realized that he could name each one of them from the grainy photographs that he had seen in the local West Palm Beach newspaper. He had followed the gang's exploits in the local news for years and had secretly admired their exploits and bravado. He also had told Martha that he hoped that he would never run across them! But here they were, near his groves. There was John, Clarence Middleton, Ray Linn, and Roy "Young" Matthews. The young wounded man was Hanford Mobley, John's nephew and the youngest member of the gang. Each man was a hardened criminal who had seen serious prison time and had escaped, and they all had a cold, desperate look about them. John continued speaking in that same calm voice.

"Levi, its mighty nice meetin' ya. I need to ask you a favor. We got a man that's hurt, you know, wounded in a little dis'greement. Hanford's in a might of pain and could use some clean bandages. Also, we are plumb starvin', and could sure use some good home cookin' to fill our bellies. If'n you can help us out, Levi, I'll make it worth yer while. Folks around here help each other out, ya know?"

"Yes sir. If'n you let me go, I'll be back in an hour with grub and clean cloths fer yer man over there."

"I need to know that I can trust you, Levi. Remember what I said."

He then did something that Levi would never forget. He raised his hand and pointed his index finger at Levi with his thumb sticking straight up like a gun. He sighted down it with his one eye and made a playful little "blam" sound. He followed this with a wink and that confidant smile. Levi's blood ran cold.

"Yyyess, sir. I'll be back directly!"

Levi hurried back to his house and told Martha about the men and who they were. Martha was shocked, but

215

understood, as he did, what they needed to do. The Ashley gang had a reputation for not only helping local folks, but also for exacting ruthless vengeance on whoever crossed them. She quickly made sandwiches and put some oranges and grapefruits into a basket while Levi gathered some rags and salve. Almost as an afterthought, he grabbed his old banjo and slung it over his shoulder by the worn leather strap.

Notorious

Everyone knew about the Ashley gang. Their exploits were known far and wide throughout Florida. John Ashley had been a common woodsman and trapper who had been accused of murdering his friend and companion, a Seminole Indian by the name of DeSoto Tiger, in the everglades. Two Palm Beach County Sheriff's Deputies were sent to arrest him, but were overtaken by John and his cohorts. They were sent back to Sheriff George Baker with a message.

"Tell him not to send any more chicken-hearted men or they might get hurt."

John had first taken flight into the depths of the Florida wilderness, then on to Seattle. He disappeared from sight for a few years, but had experienced either a change of heart or a bout of homesickness and had come back to turn himself in to Sheriff Baker. Right before his trial, he experienced another change of heart and escaped from custody yet again by climbing a ten foot fence. The officer that he had escaped from was none other than the son of Sheriff Baker, Deputy Robert Baker. This made the battle between the Ashley's and the Baker's a personal one. John and his gang started on the rapid descent into infamy by recruiting a gang of convicts, family members, and wanderers. Together they began committing a series of often violent crimes ranging from bank robbery to bootlegging.

While robbing the bank in the small coastal town of Stuart, John had been badly injured by an accidental shot from the gun of one of the gang members at that time who called himself "Kid" Lowe. This injury cost him his left eye and was so severe that he was soon captured again and sentenced to a very long stint at Raiford State Prison. Right after the trial, his brother, Bob, made an insanely brazen, yet unsuccessful, rescue attempt in the streets of Miami and was killed by police in a bloody shootout.

John's murder charge in the DeSoto Tiger trial was dropped, but he was sent to Raiford for his other crimes and, within three years, allowed to work on a road gang for his "good behavior." This was apparently part of his plan because he soon escaped again. He went back to his hometown area south of Stuart where he lived as an outlaw and a prosperous bootlegger for a few years. He and his two brothers ran illegal booze from British warehouses in Bimini and the Bahamas until John was re-captured by police during a "delivery" in Wauchula, Florida. He was immediately sent back to Raiford to continue his now extended sentence.

Amazingly, John Ashley escaped from Raiford State Prison yet again. Soon the gang was back together and ready to make a big score. The newspapers had played up John's reckless stunts, as well as his blood feud with Sheriff Baker.

Levi hurried back and gave the supplies to the gang. John seemed to be very grateful. They ate the sandwiches and the oranges like hungry wolves. When they were done, John stood up and raised his hand as if making a speech.

"I would just like to say that Levi here, bein' of sound mine and body, has done us a wonderful justice today. I declare that he is my friend!"

A glass jug of moonshine was produced and Levi was led over to the fire. Several hours later, he was completely drunk, playing his banjo and singing for the men as they howled with laughter. They all sang the words to "Bonaparte's Retreat" together and, at the conclusion of the sung fell into raucous laughter. Levi was in his glory as the consummate entertainer. He was having fun with these men.

"Levi, yer allright!" John laughed, "I declare, I ain't seen nobody as funny as you!"

"Well thank you sir!" Levi woozily saluted him as if John were a military officer.

"I want to hear somethin' sad, Levi. Play me a real tear jerker," John said.

Levi thought for a moment, and then started to play a haunting roll on his banjo. He sang in a soft voice.

"I am a poor wayfarin' stranger

travelin' through this world below

There is no sickness, toil, or danger

In that fair land, to which I go

I'm goin' home to see my mother

I'm goin' home, no more to roam

I am just goin' over Jordan

I am just goin' over home."

Levi finished, and looked up. All of the men were very quiet. John was sitting in his place on the other side of the fire. Levi was shocked to see that the man's face was streaming with tears. Levi quickly looked down, embarrassed. John spoke in a quiet voice.

"Levi, that song was my granddaddy's favorite. He told me that it was about a lost soul, searchin' for somethin' that he lost along the way. That's gonna be me soon."

Nobody said a word for a few moments, until Middleton broke the silence.

"Not me. I'll be here drinkin' corn whiskey when y'alls six feet under."

The entire group, including Levi, erupted in laughter.

Later, Levi sat by the fire and listened to the men talk. Middleton grew very serious.

"You know, Sheriff Baker's gonna come after you like hell on wheels after that fiasco yesterday. I guarantee he ain't happy about you killin' his cousin."

"Yea, well an eye fer an eye, I say. That sumbitch shot my Daddy. I'll kill him for that someday," John answered with a growl.

"I just wish you hadn't a gone and made it so personal with them law boys. They can make it very bad fer us. You shouldn't have left that bullet for the Sheriff back in Pompano."

At this, John showed his wide, boyish grin. "You didn't like that, Clarence? I thought that was a nice touch. I guess me and Bob's little blood feud just turned up a notch."

Middleton smiled at John. "Sherriff Baker says he's gonna pull that glass eye out of yer head and wear it around his neck fer decoration!"

The men all howled with laughter at this.

Later on the men grew quiet, and one by one got up and staggered to the small building to sleep.

Levi staggered into the house obscenely late that night to a very angry, but relieved, Martha.

Levi later learned that the very day before he had met them, the Ashley's had been involved in a bloody, heated shootout with law enforcement in South Stuart in which John had killed the cousin of Sheriff Baker, Deputy Fred Baker. This was touted by John as "revenge" over the killing of his father, Joe Ashley.

Two days later Levi headed back to the shack. He had gathered up his courage and wanted to have a look around. The gang had cleared out, so he went inside. There were bare furnishings; a table, three chairs, a dresser, and three moth ridden cots on the floor. Levi walked over to the dresser to inspect the contents of it. As he crossed the rough plank floor his boot caught something and nearly tripped him up. He looked down and noticed that something didn't seem quite right. The pattern of the floor was wrong. He got down on his knees and pulled at what appeared to be a loose board. He lifted it up and found that it was a two by two foot section of planking. He looked down into the darkness of the space below. Was something down there? He reached in and felt something smooth. He grabbed it and pulled it up. It was a mason jar, much like the ones that Martha used for canning, with a lid on it.

"Oh my God!" he said as he examined the glass jars contents.

Inside, Levi could see a large bundle of paper bills wrapped up with a string.

He whistled out loud and considered his find. He had stumbled across one of John Ashley's secret hiding places.

"If'n I take even a nickel of it, they'll plug me full of more holes than a fruit strainer." He said sadly.

He placed the jar back in its hiding place and replaced the floor boards. He left the shack and began his walk home down the trail back into the dense trees, lost in his thoughts. He never told Martha about what he had found.

On November second, nineteen twenty-four, Levi read the story in the West Palm Beach newspaper. Law enforcement officials had gained knowledge that the Ashley gang was headed north to John's sister's home in Jacksonville. They had staked out the only route north, the Federal Highway, and had set up a chain across the road at the south end of the Sebastian River Bridge. The red lantern they had hung on the chain proved to be a bad omen for the gang. No one knew what really happened, but Sheriff's deputies were rumored to have assassinated them while they were in handcuffs by the side of the road. They were all dead. Sheriff Baker laid claim to his grisly glass eye souvenir.

Levi had told his wife that he had been so disturbed by this news that he had to go for a walk that very day over to the woods north of the grove property. He ended up back at the little shack in the woods. He went inside, then emerged a few minutes later, a hurried pace in his step. He walked down the trail toward home. After about fifteen minutes, he paused.

He had heard a noise.

Was that whistling?

He looked around through the palmetto scrub. Seeing nothing, he shook his head and continued.

He heard it again.

Someone was whistling a tune, but he couldn't tell from what direction. It was very faint, but seemed to be coming from everywhere. Suddenly he recognized it.

"Wayfaring Stranger."

Levi felt a chill run down his spine, and he began to run down the trail.

"Cypress Reflection"- Jackie Brice

Four Years Later- 1928

The hot Florida sun beat down on the two men's backs as they worked. Levi and Enos had been clearing land just to the east of the river for two solid days now. They had been making excellent progress right up until they had encountered those strange mounds. Enos had backed away from them as if they were poison. He simply would not go near them. Levi had grown angry because he had been given explicit instructions to clear the land for more orange trees, and he didn't want to be held up with delays.

Levi knew that, over the years, grove workers had been finding all kinds of things out here. Guns, musket balls, belt buckles, swords, even bones had been unearthed. It was common knowledge among the workers that there must have been some sort of military skirmish here sometime in the past. He figured that they were probably from the Seminole wars that had been fought in this area. He and Enos had argued over this subject. Enos had tried to tell him that many of the Seminoles were as black as he was. Levi had laughed at this. Who ever heard of a black Indian?

"Weren't most of those battles fought further north, like up around Ocala?" Levi had asked Enos.

"Don't nobody know fo sure. All I know is, somethin' happened right here, and it was big."

All of the relics had been stored in a couple of buildings over by the barns. It was an unspoken rule that these items were not to be discussed. It was almost as if there was some sort of "taboo" about the subject. Times were very tight since the twenty-six hurricane had killed over three hundred people in Miami. People were moving north in droves, so

Levi figured that the locals who lived in this area were worried about the attention that the discovery of some sort of historic battlefield would bring to property out here. The groves and the surrounding farms were money makers in this part of South Florida. Oranges grown out here had won first prize at a big St. Louis exhibition a few years back. They had been rated as "superior" by the judges. Any outside attention to the land was seen as a threat to the livelihoods of everyone out here.

On this hot August afternoon, both men stood contemplating the two raised areas by the river. The more they looked, the more evident it became that they were not natural formations. It didn't make sense; what would have caused the ground to swell like that? Enos stared at them, shaking his head slowly.

"Uuuh Uhh." He said softly, as if to himself. It was evident that his uneasiness was growing. Levi looked at the stubborn expression on the black man's face.

"What in blue blazes is eatin' ya, Enos? You act like you seen a ghost or somethin'! Git on over here and help me clear this!"

"Nosir. I won't do it. Dem's burial mounds. Sacred. Dey's folks buried in dose mounds, Levi." He said in a low voice.

"Well, I reckon they won't mind some sweet oranges growin' out of them, now would they, Enos? That stuff makes great fertilizer anyway!" Levi cackled.

Enos just gave him a stern, serious look.

"No." He said stubbornly, and turned around to walk away.

"Christ almighty, Enos!

Enos shook his head and began to walk away.

Levi called after him, "Enos! My own grandfather was kilt down here somewhere back in the Indian wars! If'n you think anyone would be offended at digging up stuff, it would be me! Come back here and help me!"

Exasperated with his friend's stubbornness, Levi set about the work of clearing a small group of fairly good sized oak trees himself. He chained one of his mules to the trunk of one of the larger trees and started to dig around the roots of it with his shovel.

"Go on!" he shouted at the beast as the tension in the chain went taut. The tree creaked as its roots started to pull slowly from the sandy soil. He watched as they began to give way and the top of the tree slowly lowered, its branches making contact with the ground. The large jagged hole in the sandy earth that was left went fairly deep below the surface.

"That's it, girl." Levi said to the mule as he patted its rump. He led it over to the brush pile and unchained the tree next to it. Pausing to pull his handkerchief out of his pocket and wipe the sweat from his brow, he ambled back to the hole and peered inside. Something didn't look quite right. It was a bone. He looked at it closer and could see that it was too small for a cow. It appeared to be a leg, or maybe an arm bone. He got an unsettled feeling as he realized that it was most likely human. He stood for a moment gazing at it as he pondered what to do. He spat some tobacco on the ground and climbed into the hole with his shovel. Getting down on his knees, he set the shovel next to him and carefully dug further down with his bare hands. He had soon uncovered a skull, confirming what he suspected; that there was a full skeleton below him. He continued the work of unearthing it completely.

After an hour or so, Levi stood back and stroked his chin as he observed the pile of bones that he had found. He pulled a dirty rag from his back pocket and wiped the sweat from his forehead as he considered what to do with them. His job was to clear that land, and he did not want to upset his employer with details such as this. Stroking his chin, he considered walking back to the main house to tell the grove boss what he had found. He looked up at the glaring sun and saw that it was getting late and, surmising that he had not gotten much of anything done yet, made a decision.

Levi walked toward the edge of the river with an armload of the bones. He dumped them on the bank in a scattered pile. One by one, he tossed them into the swift current of the Loxahatchee.

"Burial at sea!" he chortled to himself as he tossed the last of them, the skull, into the water. It sunk under the surface with the impact of his throw, and then bobbed back up into view, its hollow eye sockets seeming to look at him as it floated away and out of sight.

He turned his head and happened to looked at the large oak tree with the huge spreading branches over to the west side of the grove. It grew out of a raised area about six feet higher than the ground around it. Enos had told him that it was another one of those burial mounds. Levi noticed how majestic this tree looked. It was higher than all of the others and had moss hanging down from its' branches all the way to the ground. He saw a movement in the upper branches and noticed a white flash. It was a bird; an osprey, and it seemed to be looking straight at him. He should not have been able to see its eyes at this distance, but he could. The stare was almost malevolent in its unbroken intensity. The sight unnerved him and a chill ran down his spine. He looked away, shook off the feeling and got back to work.

At the end of the day the wagon bounced over the rough road as it slowly made its way back toward home. He felt a little uneasy and out of sorts. Looking up at the darkening sky, he knew that he had dallied too long; the sun was almost down. The two old mules were plodding along at their usual slow gait, so he snapped the reins impatiently in a futile attempt to speed them up. He felt exhausted, but satisfied that he had gotten a lot done today. He was hauling a wagon full of sweet oranges, and the land that he had cleared would be a good addition to next year's crop. He reached under the seat of the wagon and pulled up the half full glass gallon of moonshine that he kept there. He uncorked it, pulled it over his shoulder and, turning his head, took a good swallow from it.

"Mmmama!" he said, smacking his lips.

He attempted to cheer himself up by thinking of how surprised his wife was going to be when she found out what he had planned for the family. He had already made the down payment on the truck, and he would be able to pick it up next month. After that, he would go tell the grove management what he thought of them, and then quit his job. He would then buy his own piece of land and grow his own oranges. He had bided his time until it was right, and the hour was quickly approaching. Nothing could stop him now. Between the money that he had gotten from the Ashley hideout and the little bit that he had been putting away these last few years he almost had enough to do it. He had been afraid to tell anyone about the Ashley money until things had definitely blown over.

"Them son's a guns been in the ground nigh on four years now," he said out loud, as if reassuring himself, "most folks have forgot them by now."

Enos had not returned today to help him. Levi was a little angry about that. He wondered why the man was so stubborn. Who cared about old bones anyway? He did not feel entirely right this evening, despite the buzzing in his head from the frequent gulps of moonshine he had been taking from the jug under his seat. He had an uneasy sense of dread that he could not get rid of.

As the wagon rounded a corner on a path that ran between two sections of tall trees, he felt a jerking movement on the right side. The wagon seemed to shift, and he saw the front right wheel hub bearing come loose and fly off, skittering away on the hard packed shell surface of the road. The wheel itself became unbalanced on the shaft for a few moments before it came loose and rolled away. He pulled at the reins in a frantic effort to stop. The wagon lurched to the right and the front corner slumped down and caught the roadbed. It started to roll over. Levi, in a panicked effort to free himself from it, jumped off the seat and away from it. He flew through the air and landed feet-first, but his left foot was not entirely straight and he felt his ankle turn before he crashed into the vegetation. His head bounced on a piece of limestone and he landed hard on his side with a painful groan.

When he regained consciousness, it was dark. He looked around and tried to remember exactly where he was. Getting to his feet, he winced in pain as he gingerly put weight on his foot and ankle. He rubbed his sore head and noticed the fullness of the moon and that he could see pretty well. He limped over to the wagon and shook his head in disbelief as he surveyed the damage. It lay overturned and broken halfway off the shell rock road. There were oranges everywhere, both smashed and whole, and the sweet pungent smell was overpowering. The reins holding the mules had ripped and broken in the tumble, so both animals stood unhurt, feeding on the dry grass by the road.

"I see you made out pretty well in the fall, you dumb asses." he said out loud.

He heard a sound. It didn't seem to come from any particular direction, but all around him.

It was a man whistling.

He recognized the tune as soon as it started.

It was "Wayfaring Stranger," John Ashley's favorite song.

His scalp tightened with fear. Levi had never believed in ghosts, or haints, as his mother had called them, but he was currently having second thoughts.

He felt the grip of panic take hold of him. Where was it coming from?

He looked around wildly. He remembered what John Ashley had told him so many years before; that the song was about him.

Then he heard another sound. This time it was a laugh.

A man's mocking laughter.

He didn't know what else to do, so he ran. He winced at the shooting pain in his ankle, but tried to run anyway in a kind of slew-footed hobble. After a short distance he began to calm down a bit, so he gave up and began to walk. He was now on the trail that ran through the trees along the west side of the river. The mid- September moon was huge and full, and its light illuminated everything. He looked up at it and saw the silhouette of a tall cypress tree, as if it were a shadow cutout on a large round piece of paper. He stopped for a moment to admire the ethereal beauty of this sight. He noticed that there was a large osprey nest in the very top of it. He remembered that he had seen this tree many times in the daylight. He could make out some movement in the top of the nest.

"Hey momma," he said softly, "I don't mean no harm to yer yungun's."

He could hear the warning cries of the bird growing louder. He looked down at the water and saw the fog that was starting to rise from its surface. He was startled when he heard the loud grunt of a pig frog, so he decided to limp on a little further, moving along the trail as swiftly and deliberately as his sore ankle would allow. The nagging feeling that something was not quite right would not leave him.

He paused as he sensed something like an electrical charge in the air, and he knew at once that he was not alone. He heard it then; a noise, a very low, vibrating tone. A small spark of panic began to grow inside him as he recognized the sound. The animal casually loped out from the trees and onto the road, its magnificent gold body shimmering in the bright moonlight. It stood about fifteen feet away directly in front of him. It looked up, and Levi found himself looking into the face of a huge Florida panther! Its amber, almost greenish eyes blazed with malevolence as it gazed directly at him, and he found that he could not look away. The creature's eyes seemed to glow with an unnatural light. Something was wrong; panthers did not act this way. There was a kind of evil intelligence in those eyes, and Levi felt his blood run cold with fear. He looked wildly around for any means of escape. He knew that panthers could be aggressive and unpredictable. The cat lowered into a sitting position and calmly stared at him, its great tongue lapping across its mouth.

From the top of the cypress tree he heard another sound; the sharp, high pitched cry of the osprey. There was a commotion of flapping wings and branches, and something swooped by his head. It came so close that he felt the breeze of it on his face and the tickle of feathers. His hands flew to his head to bat it away. He was so startled by this that he didn't know what to do, so he stood there in frozen panic and stared straight ahead.

Then he heard it…his name! It was almost imperceptible, like a whisper, but definitely there!

"Leeeeviii."

The osprey made another pass very close to him and swung down a scant few inches above the hard surface of the trail ahead, then disappeared into a thicket of palmetto on the far side of the path. Levi looked back at the huge panther.

It was gone! Vanished!

His head swung wildly from side to side as he searched for it. Levi knew that he was going to be attacked and killed right here in this spot by the river. There was no sound now, and he was sick with fear. After a few moments he started to move slowly along the trail. He strained to see what was ahead of him. His ankle was screaming with pain and he was more scared than he had ever been.

He noticed a dull light and some movement ahead a good distance up the trail. Was someone coming to help him? There wasn't supposed to be anyone out here this time of night. Levi quickly moved behind a large live oak. As he stood with his back against the tree, he could hear his own breath coming in panicked rasps and he could feel his heart pounding in his chest.

What in God's name was happening to him?

He peered around the tree's huge trunk. Whoever or whatever it was what getting closer. Levi strained his eyes in the darkness to try and identify it. He could see the light growing brighter as it bounced through the trees ahead and closed the distance between them. He pulled his head back and listened for the sound of footsteps. Not hearing anything, he peered around the tree again into the darkness. He could now make out that the source of the light was a person moving quickly toward him through the woods. He ducked back, hiding himself.

Shaking with terror, he slowly moved his head around the tree and looked. It was closer, and Levi could see that it was a man, and he seemed to be running. Strangely, there was no sound! All he could hear was the constant ringing drone of the cicadas in the trees. Normally, you could hear a man running through the woods at least a half mile away! Levi pulled his head back and stared straight ahead, feeling nauseous with fear and dread. After a few moments he sensed something to his right and slowly turned his head. What he saw nearly caused him to faint.

It stood on the trail facing him. The figure glowed with an unnatural light like a lantern. It had once been a young man, more like a boy, dressed in the ragged and torn uniform of a soldier, but not a modern one. It was a fighter of old, and appeared to be drenched and dripping with river water. It was nearly transparent, as if made from the thinnest of parchment, and Levi could see completely through it at the trees and bushes behind. Its face bore a haggard expression that seemed to be a combination of confusion, anger, and fear. On its head it was an ancient leather forage cap that had once held its shape, but now sat in a crumpled heap, only being held in place by a leather strap under its chin. It wore a high collar tunic with straps crisscrossing its chest. In one hand it carried an ancient musket of some sort, its stock completely eaten away to nothing from years in the water.

Its eyes were black, empty spaces that seemed to have no definitive edges, but were constantly moving and reshaping. As Levi looked into these dark chasms, he experienced a sense of sadness and loss that seemed to have no limit. It was as if the spirit had injected these feelings into his soul. Levi's eyes welled with tears, and he felt a confusing wave of terrible memories that were not his own assault his mind. He saw the face of a very young woman, probably Indian, with terrified eyes. He then saw a different face, a black man like Enos, the eyes filled with intense hatred and anger.

Levi broke his gaze with the phantom and both the images and the sorrowful impressions immediately disappeared. He shrank back in fear and futilely tried to disappear behind the tree. The specter just stared at him for a few moments, cocking its terrible head slightly as if inquiring about something. Just as he knew that the ghost boy was going to kill him, it slowly turned and began to run back toward the river, its footfalls making no sound whatsoever. He watched in terrified fascination as it stopped at a point about fifty yards past him. It then turned and walked down the river bank to the water, not stopping at the water's edge, but continuing right into the blackness of the river. There was no splashing sound around the figure's legs. All Levi could see was the top half of its body above the thick cloak of fog.

Levi was beyond panic. He had entered into a state of shock.

The figure walked four or five feet into the river and stopped. It raised its head and seemed to be looking at the far bank of the river. A few moments passed and, very suddenly, it threw its hands up in to its head as if struck by something. It opened its mouth as if screaming in pain, but

243

there was no sound at all. Then it fell sideways into the fog and disappeared below it without a sound or splash.

Levi stared in disbelief and horror at the foggy river. At least an hour passed before he gathered himself. He heard nothing now and saw no spirits, so he hobbled the last half mile toward home as fast as he could.

"What in God's name is happenin' to me? I don't even believe in haints, but these durn groves is plumb full of 'em!" he mumbled to himself as he moved along.

"What the matter, Levi? What happened? Where's the wagon?" Martha peppered him with questions.

Levi raised his hand with his palm facing her and said, "No questions just yet, woman. I cain't catch my breath."

He leaned over, his hands on his knees and gasped in ragged, deep breaths. After a time he raised his eyes to hers. She could see that he was badly scared.

"What in God's name got into you, Levi McCracken? You're pale as a ghost!"

"I think I seen plenty this night!"

Her honest look of concern transformed to one of incredulousness, then skepticism.

"What are you talkin' about?"

In a quavering voice, he told her what had happened to him out on the main road. Her expression turned to one of anger.

"Have you been in the hooch again, Levi? You been getting' liquor from gangsters and bootleggers again?"

"No, Martha, no, I'm tellin' you, I seen it. The bird called out my name!"

Martha shook her head and turned away. She went into the bedroom and slammed the door. Levi knew that it was hopeless to share this with her. He rolled himself up on the couch and closed his eyes. He was alone in this one.

The Storm

A few days later, as he drove his newly repaired wagon in from the groves, Levi looked out over the long rows of orange trees at the dark clouds gathering in the distance. He was tired from the nightmares he had been experiencing since that terrible night and his encounter with the phantom soldier. Those terrible cavernous eyes were still fresh in his memory. Breathing in deeply, he could smell the moisture in the air. The temperature had dipped a few degrees, and he could feel his ears popping as the air pressure dropped ever so slightly. He felt a twinge in his knee, so he rubbed it with his right hand as he held the reins with his left. All day long the grove workers had talked about the weather that was coming. They all thought that the conditions were ripe for a bad storm. Enos had told him that he could smell and feel it coming, and his predictions were usually dead on. It had been a hot mid-September day in the groves, so the cool air was welcome, but he had a slight sense of apprehension that he couldn't shake. He knew that he had better get home quickly.

When he got to the house he tried to hide his unease from the family, but failed.

"Why do you keep lookin' out the window, Levi?" Martha asked.

"No reason. I'm just keepin' an eye out at the weather. There may be some rain and wind comin' our way this evenin'."

Her silence spoke volumes. After a few moments she spoke.

"Just how bad a storm you thinkin'?"

"Don't worry Martha. We'll be fine. Remember that storm back in Tennessee in seventeen?"

Patrick S. Mesmer

She smiled at him and said, "We nearly near lost the house in that one."

"That's right," he said in his best soothing voice, I'll keep an eye on it through the night. If it gets worse, I'll board the windows."

He knew that it was the peak of hurricane season and that a terrible one had blown through South Florida only two years before. The "Great Miami Hurricane" devastated the Miami coast and had taken over three hundred lives. An estimated forty-five to fifty thousand people had been rendered homeless in the storms aftermath. Not only had the storm taken its toll in human lives, but it also devastated the local economy. The grove had experienced a conspicuous decline in business since it had happened.

Later that night, after everyone had turned in, Levi's eyes snapped opened. He was covered in sweat and could not focus, and for a few confused moments didn't know where he was. He realized that it was only another nightmare. He had once again been running from phantom panthers and ghost soldiers in his dreams.

He looked around the small bedroom and out the window, and saw that the three coconut palm trees in the yard were swaying with more force than usual. The wind was whistling against the rough edges of the siding, and he realized that it had started to pick up significantly. He rose from bed, walked to the window, and looked out.

"Levi? What are you doing?" Martha asked him.

"I'm gonna go board up. I don't like the way the wind sounds."

He pulled open the bedroom door and stepped into the front room, quietly closing it behind him. He reached for his jacket on the hook by the door, slipped it on, and plopped his old hat on his head. As he opened the front door and stepped out onto the porch, the warm, humid wind hit his face immediately. He sat down on the porch rocker and began massaging his right knee as he tried to gather his thoughts. He should have listened to his intuition and his sore knee. His knee had been warning him of bad weather his whole life. He reached underneath the rocking chair and pulled out the whiskey jug. He uncorked it and took a good pull, the liquid burning his throat as it went down. He felt better already.

An hour later he woke from his sleep with a start. He realized that he was still sitting on the rocker on the front porch. He saw that the weather had rapidly deteriorated in a very short time. He had fallen asleep when he was supposed to be boarding the windows up. The wind was starting to wail and the ominous gusts were starting to blow. The fronds of the coconut palms were bouncing wildly in unison. He could definitely feel the pressure dropping in his ears, and his knee throbbed.

The wind howled, and the rain had started pelting against the side of the house. The gusts were coming with steadily increasing ferocity. He got up from the rocker and made his way down the steps and across the yard to the barn, holding his old hat to his head with his hand. The driving rain and darkness made it hard to see. He forced the large doors open and slipped into the darkness of the barn, the wind slamming them shut behind him. He could hear the nervous nickering of the mules in the rough stalls. The wind and rain rattled the shingles of the roof and the old building groaned and creaked. He stumbled to the rear of the barn and picked up two long rough- hewn boards, then made his way back toward the doors and the rainy darkness.

He heard something that sounded like a voice calling out his name. It was a strange sound because it seemed to be almost part of the wind.

"Leeeevi, why?" were the nearly unrecognizable words. They were soft as a whisper, but screaming like the storm.

He stopped and cocked his head in disbelief, and immediately flew into a rage. "You haints agin! Leave me alone!"

Then he heard what sounded like a woman's laughter.

He shook his head as if to rid himself of the sound and made his way back to the large doors. He dropped the boards and pushed them open, but the wind and rain were increasing minute by minute and pushed them back at him. He picked up the planks and threw them, one by one, out into the yard. As he exited the barn, the large doors slammed shut with such force that it shook the whole building. He grabbed the boards and was nearly blown over by a strong gust as he crossed the yard to the house. He climbed the porch, and tripped over himself as his foot caught the edge of the top step. He stumbled forward and dropped the boards on the wooden porch with a loud crash. He ran to the south end of it and pulled up the lid of a hinged wooden box, grabbing the hammer and a can of large nails inside it. He ran back, snatched up one of the long boards, and made his way down the steps and around to the west side of the house.

It surprised him how fast the wind was rising, and he cursed out loud as he pushed against its force. He could hear a roaring in the distance that sounded like a large freight train. He approached the largest window and, with one hand, tried to hoist the board over it. With his other hand, he reached into the can for some nails. Suddenly, a strong blast of air got under the board and pulled it away from the window, nearly hitting him and causing him to lose his balance. As he fell to the muddy ground face first, his hat flew off his head and blew away.

"Dad gum it!" He screamed out loud.

The storm was getting even stronger, and the rain pelted his face. He got up to his knees and made his way back around to the front of the house, slipping and sliding on the muddy ground. He made his way up the stairs and back inside. Martha and the children were huddled in the corner staring at him with fear in their eyes.

"It's no use, Martha. You and the children will have to go," he announced to his family, "I reckon this storm's gonna be too much for this place."

Martha gave him a pleading look.

"Levi, we can't go! What will we do? What about the children?"

"Listen to me, woman! I seen storms the likes of this before! There ain't a safe building around!"

"Where will we go, Levi?"

The children were starting to cry. Another great blast of wind hit the house, and Levi heard the frame of the building creak and moan.

"You hear that? The worst of it ain't even here yet!"

He could have sworn just then that he heard his name in the crying moan of the wind. His mind raced for a solution.

Then he remembered something.

"That's it!" he exclaimed. "Gather up the young'uns!"

The family left the little house in the wet darkness. The wind was blowing in very heavy gusts now and the sky was a great black swirling mass with no stars or moon in sight. Branches blew by, along with small crates, planks, signs, and many other projectiles. The family made their way along at a slow but steady pace, walking in a tight cluster along the dirt road between the rows of orange trees.

"The Celestial Railroad"- Library of Congress

Shelter and Retribution

The storm had not yet reached full force, so they were drenched but unharmed when they reached the abandoned railroad car surrounded by trees that the grove owners had bought and put here as a temporary shelter for the migrant hands during harvest season.

255

This was one of the original passenger cars from the old "Celestial Railroad" that had run from Jupiter to Juno back in the eighteen nineties. Henry Flagler's Florida East Coast Railway had put it out of business, and the grove owners had bought the passenger car at public auction in June of eighteen-ninety six. It had sat here for thirty-two years undisturbed and rusting away. It was about twenty-five feet long and had eight windows along each side of it. Several of the windows were broken, but there were enough left intact to keep out the driving rain. Through years of neglect a few stout palmetto trees had grown close around the railroad car on three sides creating natural support against high winds.

Levi climbed the small steel platform mounted to the car's side and turned the corroded handle. He pulled on it with all his might and, with a loud creak, the rusted door opened.

"Come on, git in!" he hollered to his wife and children. One by one they entered the dirty space.

The entire middle section of seats had been removed. The car was well built and very heavy, so Levi felt that it would be much safer than their rickety, wood frame house.

"Well," Martha said, "at least it's safe and mostly dry."

"That's right!" Levi said, "It'll take a strong gust to blow this over. You youngun's make yourselves ta home."

The wind pushed against the side of the car, making it rock back and forth a bit, but it seemed to be very sturdy with the added support of the palm trees. Levi lit a small kerosene lamp that he had brought and placed in a dry corner. It didn't emit much light, but it was enough to see. Martha laid out some of the damp blankets, and she and the children wrapped themselves up in them.

Levi had the nagging feeling that something was not right.

"I know I plumb forgot somethin', Martha. I cain't for the life of me remember what it is," he said as he paced back and forth.

Outside the wind roared like a locomotive. The gusts were frightening in their intensity, and every time one pushed against the wall of the railroad car it lifted off the ground slightly on one side. It was very frightening to the little family. They could hear trees splitting in pieces and flying objects smacking into the side of the car.

Suddenly, Levi remembered. It hit him like a ton of bricks. The money in the fireplace!

"Gall dang it!" he suddenly howled.

"What in God's name is wrong, Levi?" Martha shouted.

Levi punched the wall of the car with his fist.

"I got to go back to the house!"

"What? Have you lost your cotton pickin' mind, Levi?"

"I got to go back to the house!" he said again.

"Levi, the house may not be there now! You said so yourself!"

He walked to her and took her by the shoulders.

"Martha, I love you so much, but I got to go back to the house! There's somethin' I plumb forgot!"

Levi had never told his wife about the money in the fireplace, so he seemed quite insane to her now.

"Levi, you have finally lost your senses. The liquor has taken you."

Martha was getting angry. The rain that was pelting the side of the railroad car was so loud that they could barely hear each other.

"If'n I go now I'll be back in less than an hour!"

"You may be dead by then!"

"I have to go!"

With that, he pulled the door of the car open and disappeared into the darkness of the hurricane.

"Damn fool!" his enraged wife screamed as she pulled the door closed, then pounded it with her fists.

She turned to the children, who were so shocked by their father's erratic behavior that they couldn't say a word. Martha realized that they looked like homeless little waifs in their wet blanket. She burst into tears and went to them.

"He'll be back. I promise." she said to them as she gathered them in her arms. They lay huddled together in the corner of the abandoned railroad car and listened to the raging hurricane outside.

Levi held his head down against the wind and lashing rain as he made his way back down the grove road. He walked a few feet, then one of the gusts would roar through and he would have to stop to regain his balance. Several times he was nearly clobbered by broken branches flying and rolling wildly by. He saw a small building roll by end over end like a child's toy. He had to get down on the ground many times to avoid being knocked over by the driving wind.

After what seemed like an eternity he saw the shape of his little house in the distance. It was still there! He felt moisture around his feet and saw the he was standing in almost half a foot of water. He realized that the river had overflowed its banks. He sloshed his way toward the house just as a huge gust came through and bent all of the trees almost all of the way over at once. Levi lost his balance and fell into the filthy water with a splash. He heard a tearing, groaning sound and looked up to see the front porch of the house rip away and transform into a pile of broken boards and shingles.

"Gal dang it!" he roared at the wind.

"Leeeeevii."

It was the voice again, he thought. He whirled his head around to see where it came from.

He flew into another rage.

"Leave me the hell alone, you devil ghost! I ain't done nothin' to you!"

He heard that awful laugh again, mocking him.

He focused on the front door of the house. It was still there and still closed. He waded through the deepening water up to it. The door was about three feet up, so he had to climb up some broken framing left over from the porch to get to the latch. He pulled it open and fell inside. The wind slammed the door with merciless force, nearly splitting it. Levi looked up and tried to focus. He felt a great fatigue take hold of him as he lay on his living room floor. The walls creaked and groaned with stress as the hurricane force winds pushed relentlessly.

He then remembered why he had come. He got up to his knees and crawled to the dark fireplace. He grabbed the loose rock and worked it free. He reached inside to pull out the mason jar.

It was not there!

Rage and confusion filled his mind. Who had taken it? Who even knew it was there? It had to be Martha. She had found it and taken it from him. He would show her.

It was then that he heard a new sound. It was the sound of a man screaming. Was it the wind? No, it couldn't be, he thought.

"I thought you were my friend, Levi?"

Something to his right caught his eye. He turned his head and looked out the glassless window by the rear of the house where the porch used to be. What he saw made him scream out in shocked terror. Levi knew those features well. There was a bluish white light shining all around it. The eye patch was still in place over the left eye and stood out starkly against the pale skin of the face. The other eye was shining with a crimson red light as if from the devil himself. The face was intact, but there was a huge, gaping bullet hole in its forehead that dripped black fluid down onto its cheek. It was giving Levi that leering smile that had always reminded Levi of a wolf getting ready to devour its prey. The figure raised its hand and pointed its index finger at him with the thumb straight up like a pistol.

"Shame, shame, Levi!" it said in loud, booming voice.

Levi then saw what the spirit was holding in its other hand. It was an empty glass mason jar.

In a blind panic, Levi got up and raced for the front door. He could hear the terrible entity laughing at him as he ripped the front door open and leapt out into the storm. The water was deep now. He plunged into it and was completely submerged. He struggled and thrashed his way to the surface and gasped for breath. He was surprised to see that he was even with edge of the roof.

"Where in God's name did all this water come from?" he thought.

He flailed his arms out and gripped the gutter spout of the roof and pulled himself toward it. With a supreme effort he pulled his exhausted soaked body up onto the tin roof of the house. The hurricane raged in all of its force now and the rain pelted his skin like little spikes. He pulled himself up to the stone chimney of the fireplace and wrapped his arms around it. He closed his eyes tightly and hung on.

He heard the voice call his name. This was not the terrible voice of John Ashley. This was the other voice.

"Leeviiii."

He burst into tears. He was broken.

"Why!" he screamed, "Why me?"

"You know why, Leeevii."

"No! I don't know why! Tell me!"

That's when he saw her. She stood on the roof right in front of him, seemingly unaffected by the wind or the rain. She shone with a shimmering light, and she was transparent. She was Indian, he could see, but not Seminole. She was from some time long ago. Her rough dress flowed in the wind, but not like the hurricane winds that raged all around. It flapped as if just in a light breeze. Her arms were outstretched. He could see that, in life, she had been beautiful. Her eyes were shifting black spaces and her mouth was smiling at him. She wore a necklace of beads that Levi recognized as similar to the ones that he had found in the grave by the river. He then heard her voice, but her mouth did not move. It was all around him.

"Leeevii. You remember. You desecrated my grandfather's resting place. I wanted to take your life then, but I realized that you would serve a greater purpose. You will help me to protect this place for all eternity. This is a great honor, Levi. You will see."

Tears streamed down his face as he looked at this horrifying vision. After everything he had been through, he remembered those bones that he had tossed into the river. He thought of this as he felt the roof beginning to give way. He knew the truth as the entire structure caved in underneath him. He felt himself falling and saw the walls of the house he had built with his own hands crashing down on top of him. He felt the great weight of his own creation pushing him under the water.

He felt his body being greatly stressed, as if his limbs were being pulled in many different directions at once by a great force, and then there was peace. He felt a great lightness as he rose out of the water. He looked below and saw the crushed, drowned remains of his former self. There were many like himself floating through the night from the west. He felt strangely calm as he joined the silent procession of souls as they searched for their destination. He seemed to feel a great weariness descend upon him, and everything went dark.

He woke and saw that there was no rain. The moon was brilliant in the sky and the stars were clearer and more numerous than he had ever remembered them. He looked up and saw that his house was completely gone except for the stone chimney that stood there like a lone sentinel in an empty field. His sense of smell had become very acute, and he could sense the moisture in the air. His hearing was amazing; he heard a noise and realized that it was a squirrel darting through the weeds at least two hundred yards away. He felt strange and different, and let out a bawling howl as he felt a great hunger. He rose to his feet and began to lumber through the broken trees and debris. He looked down at his furry body and the huge claws where his hands had been. He had become a large black bear.

Epilogue

With each addition to the animal menagerie the mystery of _Locha-Hatchee_ deepens. In peaceful times, this sacred land offers not only a bounty of self- sustainable ecosystems, but also an unmatched sense of serenity. As tea colored water courses round the embedded roots of the soaring cypress, a song is created that is matched in harmony by gentle breezes echoed from the leaves of the water hickories and swamp maples. The light thrashing of the long leaf pine joins the chorus, accompanied by the soothing percussion of the sun rising cicadas. The fresh, interwoven smells of juniper, wild jasmine and citrus flower flow from the forest with the same serene tirelessness as the sinuous current of the old river itself. This place is possibly the western hemisphere's closest comparison to the storied Garden of Eden with but one exception, that being its intolerance of conflict.

Throughout history, all humankind drawn to the river paid only the price of peace to remain, but woe to those who left that debt unpaid, for conflict of any kind could ignite the ancient river's engine of destruction and retribution. Those who the _Locha-Hatchee_ gave life to could find their existence redefined by the very evil and dark side of nature, and all gain by anyone could be lost in moments. To a select few, as in the case with our visited subjects, more would be demanded of them than simple life or even death. Their captivated eternal spirits could possess just enough energy to shape shift between the animal form they were condemned to occupy by day, to that of the fragmented and flowing remembrance of their living past by night.

Casitoa, the beautiful Jeaga princess, now the striking osprey, was unwillingly caught between two cultures attempting to possess that which defies all ownership. Her yet unfulfilled journey through the cycle of life and death is perpetually interrupted by her desire to be the sole guardian of the remains of her ancestors.

Isa, the proud black Seminole warrior now the magnificent panther, enhances in spirit what he lacked in life; power. In his animal kingdom he is unrivaled, and therefore free. Any creature that dares cross his path is subject to his mercy. He who shows respect for what Isa now protects will never know or see him, but any who dares break the unwritten code of the *Locha- Hatchee* will feel the strength of his retribution and experience the fear instilled by his regenerated form.

Willy, the reluctant soldier and unrepentant tomb raider, is now the cunning bobcat. No better spiritual vehicle could have been chosen for his restless spirit because he commits himself to constant patrolling, spying and listening. Sleek and fast, his animal form's purpose is to serve as night watchman against those who would dare disturb the ordained tranquility of the river.

Levi, the grizzled pioneer, is now the mighty bear. The lofty dreams he yearned for in his mortal existence saw near fruition in the form of the blood stained money so carelessly left behind by the notorious Ashley Gang. The undisputed power of the *Locha-Hatchee* chose to transform Levi into a clumsy, eternally famished brute. His never satiated appetite for personal gain serves as a lesson that, by design, we are supplied with our needs and possessed by our wealth.

Collectively, these stories showcase the *Locha-Hatchee's* seemingly supernatural ability to maintain order and discipline through the fusion of nature and spirit. Standing in observance of the passionate display of human and natural interaction should serve to remind us of this message:

Those who attempt to lay claim to the beauty of the earth while denying its existence to others may, in fact, be sacrificing themselves to become eternal gatekeepers forever trapped in a form chosen by, and which best suits, our creator.

The End

CONTRIBUTING ARTISTS

Theodore Morris

Theodore Morris is an artist whose work is a journey through time. He uses oil painting as a visual language to depict Florida's native cultures that have been lost in the mist of time. His realistic portrayal of these ancient people is not a romantic image, but a sensitive understanding of their way of life.

Morris works with archaeologists and anthropologists throughout the State of Florida gathering the latest information pertaining to artifacts and documentation for his oil paintings. He has spent many hours working excavations in Florida.

His works presently hang in museums, corporate and private collections throughout North America, Ireland, England, and Australia.

http://www.floridalosttribes.com/artist.htm

Jackie Brice

Jackie Brice, a native Floridian, is an award winning professional artist who has been painting since 1967. She studied for 11 years with her mentor and friend, A.E. Backus. Prior to her work with Backus, she studied for 10 years with Vela Boss of Miami, Florida. Ms. Brice has been invited to speak in many cities, including Jacksonville, FL, Vero Beach, FL, Denver, CO and Los Angeles, CA. She has traveled to the Loire Valley in France to study and paint the landscape of the countryside. Believing strongly that the greatest teaching tool for a landscape artist is painting outdoors, she has used this practice to capture the essence of Florida.

http://www.jbriceoriginaloils.com/default.htm

Dave Geister

Dave has worked for several years as a historical artist and illustrator and his paintings have been featured in *The Military Collector and Historian*, *The Saturday Evening Post* and several issues of *The History Channel Magazine*. His illustrations can be found in the Sleeping Bear Press children's books The Legend of Minnesota, The Voyageur's Paddle, The Legend of Wisconsin, Riding to Washington, B is for Battle Cry: A Civil War Alphabet, written by his wife Pat Bauer, and S is for Scientists: A Discovery Alphabet. The Minnesota Historical Society and many other state and county historical societies have called upon Dave's skills as a historical artist and interpreter for their sites. He can occasionally be glimpsed in costume portraying the frontier artists Seth Eastman or George Catlin. Dave appeared as Eastman in the award-winning

Twin Cities Public Television documentary, "Seth Eastman: Painting the Dakotah." and even in an episode of Oregon Public Television's "History Detectives".

Dave lives in Minneapolis, Minnesota with his dear wife and stepdaughters, Eva and Allison, who share his love of history and art.

http://www.davidgeister.com/artist.html

Marion W. Hylton

Born on a farm near Prairie du Chien, Wisconsin, and lived from about age ten in St. Paul Minnesota, Marion W. Hylton has been an active painter most of her life, and works in the realistic tradition. Her formal art training began at the Ringling School of Art in Sarasota, Florida, where she was the recipient of a 4-year scholarship. There she studied with Hilton Leech, the renowned watercolorist for whom an art center in Sarasota was named. Besides watercolor, her recent work, primarily landscapes and portraits, has included oil, acrylic and pastel, all of which are of equal interest to her.

http://www.marionwhylton.com/

Patrick S. Mesmer

BIBLIOGRAPHY OF REFERENCE MATERIAL

1.   Redish, Laura- Director
      Native Languages of the Americas
      8400 Normandale Lake Boulevard, Suite 920
      Minneapolis MN 55437
      http://www.bigorrin.org/calusa_kids.htm

2.   Swanton, John R. Access Genealogy
      Source: The Indian Tribes of North America, by John R. Swanton,
      1953, Bureau of American Ethnology, Bulletin 145, US Government
      Printing Office, Washington DC.
      http://www.accessgenealogy.com/native/florida/calusaindianhist.htm

3.   Smith, Buckingham, "Fontenada Memoir"(ca.1575). Smith
      trans.,19,1854, Washington 1854, reprinted with revisions Miami, 1944
      http://babel.hathitrust.org/cgi/pt?id=mdp.39015017647234

4.   Blackard, David M. and West, Patsy, Seminole Tribe of Florida,
      "Legends" copyright 2011
      http://www.semtribe.com/Culture/Legends.aspx

5.   Motte, James Rhett "Journey into the Wilderness" University of Florida
      Press Gainesville, Florida 1963

6.   Howard, Rosalyn "Black Seminoles in the Bahamas"University Press of
      Florida Copyright 2002 by Rosalyn Howard

7.   Brown , Robin C. "Florida's First People" Pineapple Press Sarasota,
      Florida 1994- Copyright 1994 by Robin C. Brown

8.   Huntington, R.T. (Roy Theodore) – "Accoutrements of the United
      States Infantrymen, Riflemen, and Dragoons 1834—1839" Museum
      Restoration Service- Alexandria Bay New York 1916

9.   Dickinson, Jonathan, "Jonathan Dickinson's Journal" by Jonathan;
      Edited By Evangeline Walker Andrews & Charles McLean Andrews
      Dickinson (1946)Florida Classics Library 1961

10.   Hughes, Kenneth J. "A Chronological History of Fort Jupiter", Florida
      Coast Research and Publishing P.O. Box 8845, Ft. Lauderdale, Fla.
      33310 Copyright 1992 by Kenneth J. Hughes

11.   Procyk, Richard "Guns Along the Loxahatchee"Library of Congress
      Catalog Card # 99-96050 copyright Richard J. Procyk 1999

12. MacCauley, Clay "The Seminole Indians of Florida", published by the Smithsonian Institution, Bureau of American Ethnology, Minneapolis. Minn. June 24th 1884

13. Sonne, Warren "The Ashley Gang: What Really Happened" Indian River magazine .com 12/05/2007http://www.indianrivermag.com/LIVE/index.php?module=pagemaster&PAGE_user_op=view_page&PAGE_id=69

14. "The Army and Navy Chronicles-Volume VI From January 1st to June 30th, 1838 Washington City, edited and Published by B. Homans 1838 Harvard College Library Oct. 27, 1937
books.google.com/books/about/Army_and_navy_chronicle.ht

Made in the USA
Charleston, SC
15 August 2011